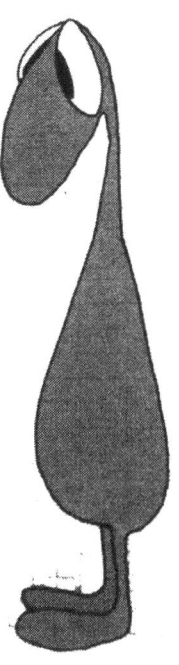

The Quest for the Magic Marble

by Refried Bean

The Quest for the Magic Marble

by Refried Bean

This book contains two collections:
At Least These Poems are Short
and *Hodge Podge*

Copyright 2016 by Refried Bean

Acknowledgements

Special Thanks to Nancy Parker and the Greenville Christian Writers Group.

Thanks also to Claire Bateman, Kimberly Gibbs, Moody Black, Wit's End Poetry, and Coffee Underground, and to Johnny Price and the Caleb Group, and to Joffre Swait.

Thank you to Jenn Cevasco, Robyn Andrews, Belinda Jenkins, Sherrie Templeton, Tyler Waddell, Mickie Belcher, Charles Dickey, Maribea Isles, Sarah and Josh Forgie, Sandra Messervy, Christina Williamson, Ginger Wilson, Joel Lakadosh, Diana Cox, Mary Stahl, Jesse Fulmer, Holly Mueller, Scott and Marianne Pitts, Paula and Barndt Benson, Maribeth Finley, Trilby Bell, Judy Martin, Beth West, Trevor, Kathy Staples, Gary Poster, and all my other wonderful coworkers and friends from Barnes and Noble.

Thank you, Connor, Katherine, Kristen, and Ava.

Thank you, Johnny C Weaver, Kimbi Mullins, Marlanda Dekine, Justin Blackburn, Mariangela Mihai, Theresa Davis, Stacie Boschma, and everyone who supported me as Psychotic Muppet.

Thanks to Catherine Polit, Charlotte Stutz, Jay Bryner, Melissa Ketchen, Beth Randolph, Wendy Mauritz, Maxi Farnsworth, Lydia Crawford, Jim Worthy, Katherine Wyma, John Cochran, Adrian Brashier, Lauren Bedsole, Hadley McCaskill, and Anne Decabooter.

Thank you Susan Mensik, Hope Cromer, Kathy Eckhart, Sergio Sanchez, and everyone at Psychiatric Associates, Upstate Psychiatry, Bay Laurel, Carolina Center for Behavioral Health, Marshall Pickens, South Carolina Research Group, and Mental Health America.

Thank you, First Presbyterian Church Greenville and First Pres Columbia, Grace Church, Woodruff Road Presbyterian Church, Fairforest Community Church, and NYU YEF.

Thank you Robert and Frances Efird, Frances Hill, Elizabeth McKoon, Doug McKoon, and thank you to Terrell Tracy, Susan Tekulve, Converse College, Bonnie Drewniany, University of South Carolina, Louise Crowley, and Vermont College of Fine Arts.

Thank you Young Life, Youthbase, Shepherd's Gate, Tina Zwolinski, and Linda Tassie.

Thanks also to the students, clients, staff, and interns at PS 132 Bronx and The Bridge.

Thank you so much, Drena Fagen, the NYU Silver School of Social Work, the Lieber Clinic, NYU Epilepsy Center and NYU Langone, Sharon Crowley, and Brian Rish.

Thank you Nicole Rivera and Cuddly Buddies, St. Mark's Vet, and Westside Vet Center.

Thank you to all my friends, family, teachers, and everyone else who has helped me.

At Least These Poems Are Short

by Refried Bean

At Least These Poems Are Short

By Refried Bean

in memory of Sheffield Wood

How to Take a Compliment

Act like you don't hear
when people tell you something nice.
That way they'll repeat it
and you'll get to hear it twice.

I'm always thinking of others.

I think of others all the time.
I do it constantly.
I think of all the selfless things
that they could do for me.

Ancient Wisdom

When you live in a house of glass
a couple things are rude:
Throwing stones is bad, of course,
and so is going nude.

Bedtime Comfort

Goodnight, my children—don't be scared.
Everything's all right.
The monster might be full
of all the kids he ate last night.

Policy

Dessert first. That's my rule.
Dessert last. Also cool.

Reminder for Aspiring Underdogs

Remember this as you go out
to overcome the worst—
To be unlikely heroes
you must be unlikely first.

Guess what I'm describing

Guess what I'm describing:
It is big and tall and blue.
It's sharp in twenty places
and it's wet with dripping dew.
It has a yellow button
and it sways from left to right
You cannot see the top except
when it's lit up at night.

Hey, really, there is no such thing.
I made it up, dear chum.
See, this was just an exercise
to make you feel real dumb.

Bad company

You're such an evil influence.
You make me do bad stuff.
Whenever I'm around you
I do not behave enough.

You're such a bad philosopher,
I'm tired of all your lies.
If I could get away from you
I'd turn out pretty wise.

You lead me into trouble
and I gossip more with you.
Alone I do not break the rules.
When you're there I sure do.

I wish you'd stay away from me.
I'm tired of this old game.
Wait, no- I guess it's kind of nice
to have someone to blame.

The Great Outdoors vs. The Great Indoors

If beaver dams are nature,
then apartments are as well.
We humans still are natural—
Just think about our smell.

How Refreshing

The gardener sprayed me with the hose.
I had no place to hide.
I smiled at him until I saw
that it was pesticide.

Dear Hallmark, I have an idea for a sympathy card:

I'm sorry that you're suffering.
You're hurting, I can see.
And from the bottom of my heart,
I'm glad it isn't me.

My Biology Class

My science class was hard.
It was a hell below all hells.
I sure found out what I am made of-
(I am made of cells)

To the Wilting Poinsetta in the E.R. Waiting Room During a Spinal Meningitis Scare

I know that you like CO_2
I recognize that most plants do
But how can you keep cheating death
by feasting on my dying breath?

Present

There's a reason to feel good right now this time today:
I'm innocent of all the sins I'll probably do someday.

Relief

You'll be quite thankful for the thrill
of having doctors laugh at you
when you go in and think you're ill
and you don't even have the flu.

The Better Than Nothin' Café

The eggs are runny. Coffee's cold.
Soda's flat here. Bread has mold.
Pie's too tart and milk is old.
Starvin's worse, though, so I'm told.

Fifty Cent Word

I'm gonna hide a fancy word within this little rhyme.
Long like banana and provocative like "time."
Well, being honest with you, it was in the second line.
I used it rather early, but I think it fit just fine.
I'll tell you what it was because I don't want to bore you.
"Provocative." What? That's not big enough for you?

Rye Pie

"Hi."
"Hi," I sigh.
"Try my rye pie."
"Why?" I pry.
"Shy?"
"Aye."
"Try."
"My, my," I lie.
"Buy!"
"Die!" I cry.
I fly.

That's What I Call Art

Your house is very lovely and my favorite thing of all
Is over here-- I love this pretty portrait on the wall.
The painting is amazing! I suspect you paid a lot.
Just look at all the detail! My, what pretty eyes she's got.

Well, goodness, I'm mistaken. I have goofed a bit I fear.
I didn't see that really this is just a mirror here.

Can People Please Give The Rhomboid The Time of Day For a Change?

I always look and look and look
for rhomboids pictured in a book.
I guess folks think that I'd be bored
by all their angles, lines, and planes
but my excitement never wanes.
The rhomboid surely sheds a tear
when overshadowed by the sphere
and other prisms greedy for
attention when they don't need more.

Genesis 2:19,20

God said to name the animals so name them all we did.
We even gave the babies names like "gosling" calf' and "kid."
Mammalia, Amphibia, Marsupials galore,
The guys down in the jungles soon will churn out more and more.
Rhachotomi and Lepospond, they've named each type of frog.
And I myself named Geraldine, my precious polliwog.

Don't Worry, Folks.

Here's my promise to the world that I will never write
a poem about used Band-Aids being looked at in the light.
I won't discuss the crusty blood that's dried and turning brown.
I'd never dare to mention yellow pus that's oozing down.
It's way too gross to write about the scabs and germs and dirt
upon the bandage you have used when you have gotten hurt.
So trust me not to list out words describing grody grime.
It's really not a subject to include within a rhyme.

Poet needed

Who will tell the story of this moss between the bricks?
Who will write some poems about these broken blackened sticks?
I am writing now about a yellow butterfly.
So who can do this other stuff? I'm sorry, but not I.

Excuse for my ignorance about certain matters

I cannot be a know-it-all
'cause that is just too tough.
And folks would rather be around
a simple know-enough.

A secret poem that is never to be read by anyone

This poem right here's a secret poem that no one is to read,
So rip it up and feel ashamed of doing your bad deed!

Sirens

Whenever I hear sirens I will say a little prayer.
I do it every time because I really really care.
If it's a fire truck's wail I hear I pray the house won't burn
and if I hear an ambulance I pray with grave concern.
If it's the cops then I will rush to get down on a knee.
and pray with all my soul that they aren't on their way for me.

Which is better?

Heroes do great things and they cannot be thanked enough.
But who deserves a bigger prize for doing something tough?
The one who serves reluctantly for duty's sake alone?
or he who does what's good because it thrills him to the bone?

Empathy

Try to walk a mile in someone else's shoes today
and don't forget that sometimes that means barefoot all the way.

Sure, I'll say the blessing

Help us act like this tastes great.
Help us not regurgitate.

To the guys who kneel in the endzones

You think you're being humble
when you give God credit due,
but it is quite a claim to say
that God takes sides with you.

Bright Side of Being Picked On

A special kind of compliment that's really pretty cool
is when you are insulted by an idiotic fool.

Fresh Starts

I've been turning new leaves over
just as fast as trees can make 'em.
I know for sure I'd hate to be
the one to have to rake 'em.

Tough Decision

God said to 40 men, "I'm gonna give you all a choice."
They trembled as they listened to His loud and booming voice.
"I know you all like goodies so I'm gonna give you some.
Just listen up and please make sure you don't choose somethin' dumb.
I'll give you forty gillion things on every single day
or just a little handful—it is up to you to say."
They all chose 40 gillion goodies (all but just one guy)
The people turned to stare at him and then they asked him why.
He said to them "I chose a handful 'cause I understand
that someone with a voice that big would have a giant hand."

More Fresh Starts

I've put all my mistakes
behind my mental cellar door
It's time to just forget them
and go try to make some more.

Getting dressed to meet my mother's friends

Stripes versus polka dots.
Which do I like best?
I like this shirt with lots of spots
but stripes are on this vest
I could just wear them both
and I've got just the thing to add
How nice I'll look with all of this
and pants of yellow plaid.

Pretty Good Deal

The world fell down but look around.
There's yellow tulips on the ground.
If earth is fallen, marred, and old
just think what heaven's yards will hold.

Hope

I saw a cockroach scurry
from the corner near my shoe
I hope it is the one I saw last night
or else there's two.

Grace Tactics

When God decides to bless someone,
he might do something wild.
He's got a bunch of options
he can use to bless each child.
He might provide a rich man
with a cellar full of wine,
or make the man so poor and thirsty
just one glass is fine.

About a quote I heard and almost fell for

"A ton of theory can't compare with just one ounce of action."
Most people read the line and then will smile with satisfaction.
But think again and see that even though this quote is fun,
it is an ounce of theory that will make you do a ton.

A Hunch

I'm understanding something that's too vague for me to pen.
But if somebody says it I will gladly shout Amen.

Trust Me

I'm good at keeping secrets. All my friends will tell you so.
Right now I'm keeping one so well that even I don't know.

Upside of Folly

It might be bad to be a fool who's cheated every day
because his soul's so good and he thinks everyone's that way.
But it'd be worse to be the scheming genius full of lies
who thinks that everybody else is also in disguise.

Don't Mention It

I always help my neighbor when I see that he's in need.
But it can take me quite a while to do just one good deed:
a minute to perform the act with just a little pout,
and up to twenty years to make sure everyone finds out.

Collection

I tried collecting stickers but I quickly gave it up.
I tried collecting glasses, too, but only found a cup.
Stamps were fun for several weeks, but then I mailed them off.
I tried collecting lozenges but then I got a cough.
Though each of my collections is the smallest in the land,
my collection of collections has grown really, really grand.

Smarts

The fancy words you learn from schools that I cannot afford
can come in very handy when you stand to praise the Lord.
But even weakest minds display some wisdom when they bow.
And who would call a man a fool who simply utters "Wow."

Body of Christ

The church is Christ's big body and each part must do its share.
But I am the appendix so I'll just relax in there.

Poem for people with short attention spans:

To show how much I care for you,
here's just two lines and now I'm through.

My Little Hobby

Most coin collectors keep their coins where they can all be seen.
But I keep mine at work inside the break room's Coke machine.

Rock Collection

Lots of Micah, Rubies: few.
Agates? Twenty. Geodes? Two.
Fossils—plenty—not all bones.
Now you say I've got gallstones?

Words of Life

A dog will take his treat to distant corners of the room
to savor it in private is his reason, I assume.
And so it is with me and nice remarks that come my way—
I'll go off with my compliment to sit and feel okay.

Thank You

People drive each other crazy
Life can be a pain.
And that is why I'm thanking you.
You always drive me sane.

Seize The Day

Evil motives, all unseen, still hide when deeds are purty.
But if we wait til hearts are clean, our hands won't ever get dirty.

I hate to be the one to have to mention this…

Gossiping 'bout Bible folks is really not so nice,
but I will still point out that someone on that ark had lice.

At the Doctor's Office

"Tell me what your symptoms are. What's putting you in pain?"
"Well, thanks for caring, doctor, but my mom said don't complain."

Bright Side

Poverty can be a gift that keeps one's errors small.
A man can't waste a million bucks if he's got none at all.

Do Not Disturb

I love to find a quiet space
To sit and stare off into space.
Whenever I can have my way
I'll sit and think the whole long day.
In fact it's odd I found the time
To come write down this little rhyme.

I don't think you understand, Doctor.

I did not come to see what pills should be upon my shelf.
I came to see how sorry I should feel for my poor self.

Consent Lament

They've jumbled up my innards and they stole my precious spleen.
And then they gave me stitches just as crooked as I've seen.
Too bad for me I signed a form that gave them all consent.
If there is ever a next time I will read the tiny print.

Bright Side

If you fail at everything
and think you won't prevail,
Take heart, my friend, because one day
You're bound to fail to fail.

Could you please talk more quietly and to someone else?

I do not want to be too rude.
Forgive me if I'm snide.
But could you please go close that door
and not be on this side?

Ice Cream Scam

McGillicutty's Ice Cream was the greatest in the land.
The flavors were superb and the ingredients were grand.
The customers would come from seven hundred miles away
His little shop was crowded almost every single day.
There was no competition. No one even dared to try.
McGillicutty's ice cream prices started getting high.
He also started skimping on the sugar and the cream.
But no one even noticed it, as wild as that may seem.
McGillicutty's product got much worse as time went by.
But customers kept buying it at prices that were high.
As long as what he sold was cold his business never hurt.
He laughed as he watched everyone eat twenty dollar dirt.

Who gets to eat this pickle?

3 Woolly Wallumps found a pickle on the street.
They couldn't quite agree on who would be the one to eat.
"Let's just have a race!" exclaimed the fastest of the three.
"No, let's see who's the strongest," said the big one happily.
The final woolly wallump picked the pickle up and cried,
"Your plans are all unfair. I know how we should all decide…
A pickle eating contest is the way that we will choose."
He ate the pickle quickly, then exclaimed, "I guess you lose."

Subverse

Fight the system, fight the man!

Let's break every rule we can!

Wait a second. Look around.

Faithful souls can not be found.

No one's doing what they should...

Let's rebel by doing good.

Lines

Oatis Henry made a living painting yellow lines.
He also did the white ones near the street lights and the signs.
Because of him the traffic flowed and people crossed the street.
The safety cops knew where to stand when they each worked a beat.

But one day Oatis Henry thought he'd paint another way
Not thinking twice about what things the mayor'd have to say.
Instead of lines he started painting hopscotch courts and grids,
Some shuffleboard for old folks and some four square for the kids.

At first there were some traffic jams on each and every day.
But then the people loosened up and went outside to play.
And if you want to know why there's no smog or filthy soot
Because of Oatis Henry this whole city is on foot.

Why do I always dream about blue flannel reindeer?

I dream of flannel reindeer
almost every single night.
The dreams fill up my heart with fear
and make me wake in fright.

They prance in rows of twenty
with no hooves upon their feet.
They're blue just like the many
on my pillow and my sheet.

Progress

You must admit that airplane food
has come a long long way.
Just these pretzels here
have flown 200 miles today.

Love Hexagon

John loves Shelia. She loves Fred.
He loves Marcy. She loves Ed.
Ed loves Courtney, She loves Chad.
Cupid's aim is really bad.

The Magic Sweater

"I love my magic sweater!" shouted little Mary Sue.
Her brother smirked and said, "What kind of magic does it do?"
"It keeps me warm when I go out so I don't get the flu.
And you are just a fool if that's not magical to you."

True Love Guaranteed

The love you get from everyone may not be real and true,
but you can make sure one thing's good, and that's the love from you.

The Company You Keep

Don't hang out with sinners. You will turn out just as bad.
You lie with dogs. You get the fleas. It's true and very sad.
So spend your time with only those who prove that they're worth knowing.
Don't ever keep bad company. Hey, wait! Where are you going?

What's That Smell?

Something smells disgusting. Something putrid fills the air.
It smells like all the eggs went bad inside the Frigidaire.
It smells like sweaty gym socks or a rotten fish filet.
I know it isn't me 'cause I just took a bath last May.

All The Right Gear

I've bought a fancy pen but I have yet to write a book.
I've bought some special pots but I am still a lousy cook.
I bought some brand name shoes but I can't dunk a basketball.
There is one thing I'm good at, though: It's shopping at the mall.

Confession

To put aside your pride
and just admit it when you fall
Is sometimes even better
than not messing up at all.

Congratulations

I'm mad that you have won this game
and shocked that I was beat.
But flattered still that you would care
enough to go and cheat.

Do you really want the hairs on your head numbered?

The pastor said, "God understands.
He knows what you are made of."
But said the culprit who had sinned:
"That's just what I'm afraid of."

Something True

It is hard to sit in gloom
with a brown dog in the room.

Of Course I Care

I'm always on my knees in prayer
(about our needy nation)
To see me not in church is rare
(that's even on vacation)
I try to get the lost in there
(to save them from tarnation)
It goes to show how much I care
(about my reputation)

Hypocrits' Defense

Our deeds are all for others' eyes. Our prayers are for their ears.
We never do what's truly good because of social fears.
But though our hollow hearts reveal that really we can't take it,
At least we care about what's right enough to try and fake it.

Habit

Doing what you're s'posed to sure gets boring every day.
With no one even looking and it's small stuff anyway.
But something huge will come along and you'll do what you should
Cause you have made a habit out of doing what is good.

Kids Today

You say our generation lacks the virtue yours displayed.
You say that we are selfish and you shake your head, dismayed.
Well aren't we all corrupt and rude, and isn't it so sad-
But don't forget that you're the ones who must have raised us bad.

News

The nasty people everywhere who do such nasty things
Might not have made those choices if they knew the wrath it brings.
And people want to share with them God's love and hope and trust,
But who will dare to share his righteous anger and disgust?

Keep the Sabbath Holy

To make each Sunday special in a vivid striking way
I'll just be extra extra bad on every other day.

Untitled

I'd trade my trophies, all my feats, my noble works and deeds,
For just a heart that's happier when someone else succeeds.

Are We Sure St. Francis Is In Heaven?

They say in heaven it's all smiles and love and brotherhood.
There won't be any poverty and that will be so good.
But let me point this out and yes, I've got a lot of nerve:
Just how can saints like him have joy with no one poor to serve?"

The Right Mistakes

Putting too much money in the church's offering plate,
Volunteering too much time with people in your state.
Forgetting to repair the sink because you're helping kids,
And making rooms too messy by recycling cans and lids.
Messing up the icing after baking Grandma's cake,
There's some mistakes you have to be quite good to ever make.

The Chicken Truck

On every day at nine o'clock,
the chicken truck drives past my block.
I see the chickens stuffed inside.
Their cages aren't especially wide.

And then at ten, I'm sad to say,
the truck drives past the other way.
The chickens all have disappeared.
It makes my stomach feel so weird.

Barnflop's Delight

Start with eggs and marmalade.
Dump in beets and lemonade.
Add some mayo. Add some salt.
It may taste bad. (Not your fault.)
Add some garlic. Lots okay?
Leave it in the sun all day.
Garnish it with fishing bait.
Chill and serve to folks you hate.

Dirt

I want the dirt on everyone. I want to know their sin.
It makes me feel much better 'bout how awful I have been.
I want to know what's wrong with every person who I see,
But that is just more dirt that every person has on me.

Don't Let The Sun Go Down On Your Anger

They say don't let the sun go down when you are really mad,
But I cannot control the sun so that is just too bad.

The Shortest Book In The World

A book about my life would be
quite fun and filled with poetry.
But if you took out all my sin
the book would be a little thin.

Etiquette For Dummies

Some people sure have social skills and wit and charm and grace.
They know just what to say when interacting face to face.
They know which fork goes where and how to dance and interview.
And how to shake your hand just right and how to party, too.
But just plain being nice can help the shyest, simple fool.
The greatest social skill there's been is just the golden rule.

Knocking

Knock and you're let in: God's hospitality is shocking.
But wilder still than that is how He sometimes does the knocking.

Secret of My Success

Today I was good but it's not cause I'm trying.
I want to sell out but there's nobody buying.

Unless I'm Mistaken

Mistakes keep people humble so I know about my fate.
If I require this many then I must be really great.

More Mistakes

If you spend your time correcting the mistakes you've made before,
it leaves a lot less time for you to mess up even more.

Bright Side

The evilest of people still can turn out pretty nice:
It takes a lot of virtue to endure a life of vice.

Don't expect me to waste a good insult.

I may not get another chance to say this thing that's wrong,
cause once we're all in heaven everybody gets along.

Good or Happy

She's always smiling, full of grace, and kind on every day.
So either she is really good or always gets her way.

Now Hiring

The devil took my resume and looked it up and down.
 He'd gone and checked my references from others in my town.
He said, "You've got experience with selfishness and vice.
You've wasted lots of time and skills. It's really very nice.
We need a girl to push a rock and push it back again.
The person chosen, sweating fire, won't stop til who knows when.
But I am sad to say my friend that though you've up and died,
In terms of getting into hell, you're overqualified.

Something To Think About As You Are Being Chased By The Paparazzi

Anonymity is great,
But then your good traits don't get known.
And fame's a blessed state
But then your dark side's also shown.

Why

When sad things happen suddenly like someone nice will die,
there's people who will say you shouldn't ever ask God why
But asking that is not a form of any kind of treason.
It's really recognition that He always has a reason.

Delusions of Nongrandeur

The lunatics get locked away for saying they're divine
and telling everybody they are God's angelic sign.
But God's own image lives in every sacred human soul,
and there's a living remnant left of what the darkness stole.
So chain the ones who say that they are part of heaven's plot,
but really all the crazy ones are those who say they're not.

Good or Bad

To bear the shame of all your wrongs and face the people still
To leave your house while knowing you don't have a perfect will
To know that you could ruin things on any given day
To know that you are evil but to live life anyway
To be with all the holy people knowing that you ain't.
Enduring as a sinner surely makes you quite a saint.

Earth Poem

Some things hurt so much that living life is hard to do,
And there is pain that makes it seem like heaven's ruined too.
But when relief and hope are far, our God might still be near.
And maybe dreams of heaven fade to help us stay right here.

Limits

When there's a huge mistake and someone stole or killed or lied,
and everyone around them is appalled and horrified,
instead of being mean to them and saying they are slime
its nice to just be glad that they aren't like that all the time.
And if they really are then let us still withhold our curse,
and just give thanks and say at least they are not even worse.
And if there's no such thing as being worse than how they are,
then let's give thanks that this world's evil only goes that far.

Provocation

The people who bring out the best in others like they should
are nice to have around because they keep you looking good.
But there is value, too, in being rattled by a foe
'cause when your darker side's exposed, well hey— at least you know.

Plea

In heaven I'll be perfect and I won't have any sin.
I'll never be annoying and I won't be rude again.
So love me now the way I am instead of getting mad,
'Cause now will be your only chance to love me while I'm bad.

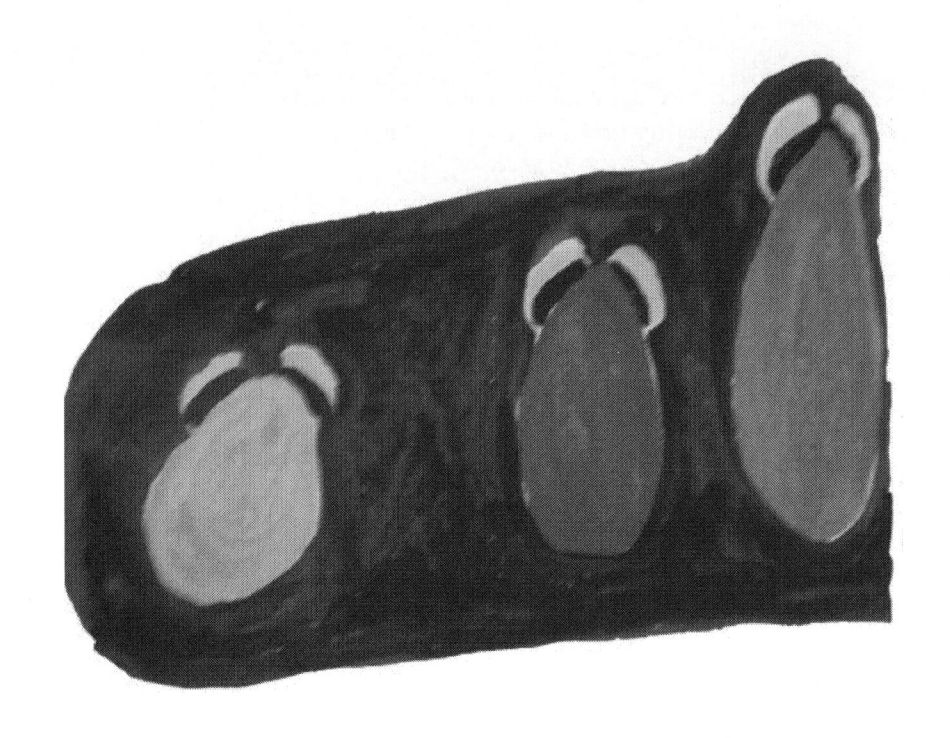

Hodge Podge

by Refried Bean

Hodge Podge

poems, stories, essays, recipes, and blog posts

by Refried Bean

This book is dedicated to the mental health field.

What you have said in the dark will be heard in the daylight, what you have whispered in the ear in the inner rooms will be proclaimed from the roofs. Luke 12:3

Hodge podge

guys what if there was a scholarship
of just love and attention
and you applied for some extra attention from teachers.

guys everything you do is going to prove the right people right

what if you thought all the stuff you said in therapy
was so good you sent the therapist a bill

Poem

I have three guinea pigs named Fred Roger and Dave.

They have very different personalities.

If I say a prayer for all the Rogers Freds and Daves of the world I wonder what will happen.

I wonder if everyone will get a little something.

A funny gag

Guys lets play a joke on God and pretend we don't like candy
but what if he says okay fine and takes it away.
nevermind.

City Counsel

guys i think that cops should wear sneakers with blue lights on them.

Maybe it is my allowance

When my friend came to visit
I had to call suicide hotlines three times
and I finally decided
that I would need to get a paycheck some day in heaven
for spending time with my friend on earth.
I told God that I charged 400 dollars a day.
That amounts to 1600 dollars
which happens to match the number
that geniuses get on the SAT.

I do not know if it means I am God's employee getting paid,
or if I am an independent contractor getting paid by a Father
who wants services for a kid. And is it a tip, or a bill, and who is
my client?

I could not figure it all out,
but I did start imagining
what I would spend the money on in heaven,
which would be pet food, books and games, and candy.

It is true that I can have that stuff now,
but it gets blocked by people
who make you have theological breakthroughs instead
so you end up thinking about the day
when people get their paychecks from the companies
in the kingdom of heaven:
the hospitals, the water company,
and the sewage treatment plant.

Basketball Tree

There was a basketball in the tree outside the school
and one of the other interns told the kids
it was a basketball tree
and I think that is enough for a poem
but some people might think the poem
needs another joke
but jokes don't grow on trees
especially not basketball trees.

Recipe poem

If people are mean to you and you curse at them in a bad way
How do you know God didn't arrange it
Because one of your rewards in Heaven
Is a cookbook with recipes based on all your sins
And there needed to be some bitterness
For a tablespoon of vinegar to put in the gingerbread cookies.

Irresistible freedom

Calvin said there's not free will.
He found Gods grace to be irresistible
and took 46 volumes to say it.
But isn't freedom grace?

Cheese grits

Strategic love to heal from senseless evil.

Senseless beauty to heal from targeted attacks

Guys what do y'all think of my new poem:

It does seem like some people have a talent for hygiene and socializing, but maybe adulthood is just my fair share of humiliation, and I can only guess that the shame I feel all the way to my scalp is there to fulfill some ancient prophecy.

Game Strategy

Guys I think it is fun in strategy games to just take a few turns and then say ok i have predicted all the possible moves and I have lost the game. Then they win the game but who seems smarter?

Guinea pig recital poem

Maybe my reward for not bringing a guinea pig to my friend's piano recital will be that in heaven some day when I give a piano recital someone actually will bring a guinea pig to mine.

Guinea pig building poem

Maybe the giant invisible cobra
hovering over the bookstore where you work
is really a giant friendly guinea pig
sitting on the roof
eating a carrot.

I think this could become one of those famous little philosophy blurbs.

What if people were told to push different buttons a thousand times not knowing what it did and then they found out that one button fed animals and one button pelted people with sharp pinecones. Should the people who fed the animals get a reward and the people who pelted people with pinecones get punished?

Blue and Green

People who have lost their marbles
should take comfort in the fact
that everyone has one big marble
which is the globe.

Young Adulthood

My 20s were hard for me
And that is why if I find out
that someone is 25 years old
I call an ambulance.

Teaching Strategy

Maybe it's not a total loss
For a whole generation to ruin everything
and tell the next people
"we should have done what we were supposed to."

Getting Old

People want me to be mature
but there's nothing in adulthood for me
and I know it and they know it
and that is why they want me to grow up.

Warthog poem

Are people still mad at me
Because Jesus Christ provided me with a pink polo shirt
with a warthog on it
when I was in high school
People might say hey you don't deserve that shirt
because you are a sinner
But what am I supposed to wear instead?
some kind of hamburger place uniform
and smear ketchup on myself whenever a child's balloon pops?
I'm wounded!

Suicide note poem

Guys I just realized today that I might have left a suicide note in a copier at the copy store back when my friend did that project on depression and I made a copy of an old suicide note for her it said I am so sorry I am so sorry and I think whoever found it probably worried and to me that is kind of funny to think about and you might say who do you think you are to just say a memory and call it a poem well I am so sorry I am just so so sorry.

People can tell

People can tell when you are only friends with them
because you know they are going to be a pirate king in heaven.

Cello Day

Something about the way
the guy played the cello in group therapy
helped me finally be able to tell the group
that I wish I was a muppet.

Babette's Feast Feast

"Fifi, what are you bringing to the Babette's Feast party?"
"Caviar."
"What?! No, really, what are you bringing?"
"I'm bringing caviar. That's what's in the story."
"We don't have to bring exactly what's in the story. Professor MacDoogenheimer said people can just bring a bag of chips if they want."
"I know. But I want to bring caviar."
"Ok," said Sheila. "I guess the lemon cookies I am going to bring won't seem that great now."
"They'll be fine," said Fifi, flipping through her notebook and looking at the notes she took about Isak Dinesen's short story. She and Sheila were sitting in her dorm room between classes. Fifi didn't really need to look at her notes, because she had been thinking about the story nonstop since reading it. In the story, Babette, a mysterious visitor to a very strict religious community, wins a huge amount of money in a contest and decides to spend the whole amount on an extravagant feast for everyone instead of buying her own escape to a more comfortable life and location.
Fifi felt inspired by the story, and was especially excited when her teacher suggested that the class have their own "Babette's feast."

On the day of the feast, Fifi and Sheila walked into class, and there were tables set up with roast beef biscuits, chicken fingers in heated containers, bottles of sparkling grape juice, French pastries, and of course, the caviar. Professor MacDoogenheimer was standing near the door, and with a nervous look said, "Fifi, did you arrange this?"
Fifi said "I sure did, Professor MacDoogenheimer."

Professor MacDoogenheimer started crying. "Fifi, all of the classes in this building have tables of food like this. What is going on?"

"It's not just this building, Professor MacDoogenheimer. I arranged for every class in the school to have a Babette's feast. This isn't even all of it. Some donuts should be here soon."

"Fifi, I just don't know what to say. This must have cost thousands of dollars."

"It did," said Fifi. "I spent my student loan money on it. It cost 40 thousand dollars. There are tables set up in the streets, too, for everyone. I do not intend to finish school."

"What?"

"I feel like reading this story was enough for me."

"Fifi! You could go to jail for misspending your student loan money! Or for not paying it back!"

"That is ok with me," Fifi said, picking up a plate and starting to serve herself some food. "Maybe some people in charge of the jail will also read the Babette's Feast story and buy us some donuts."

Art Therapy Story

"Hello?"

"Hi, is this Ralph Ralpherson? The artist?"

"Yeah this is Ralph."

"Hi, my name is Rufus. I'm an art therapist and I saw one of your paintings in a restaurant over on 6th avenue and I wanted to see if I could talk to you about it."

"Sure, which painting is it?"

"It is the train station painting over at the Waverly Restaurant."

"Oh sure, what about it?"

"Well can I talk to you in person about it at the restaurant?"

"Okay."

The two guys met at the restaurant for breakfast the next Saturday. They sat in the booth near the painting.

"Ralph, thanks for meeting with me. I want you to know that I am really sorry about what happened to your family."

"How do you know what happened to my family?"

"Well I can tell by the storefront angle and this bridge right here that your dad got caught stealing cars when you were in tenth grade. And your mom got fed up with it and told him to leave. But then she got hurt in an accident at her work."

"That's all true but I don't see how you can tell."

"Well see these birds here in the corner and the way that one bird is flying near this sign? And the way the people are waiting but this guy's newspaper doesn't have any words on it? All of that wouldn't be there unless you had an emotional block because of a sudden attachment barrier based on some kind of external shame trigger related to parent conflict. And this car right here in the corner, the way the fender color fades, it's a classic Rogerian paradox. You got an 87 on your American history final exam that year."

"That's right! I did!"

"And it looks like you talked about this in counseling when you were twenty-five. I don't think you would have used four different shades of green if that were not the case."

"Yeah I got some help. I'm doing okay now, or at least I thought I was."

"Actually, you may still benefit from some therapy. Just to talk about the grocery store thing and the radio."

"Wow okay, sure. Thank you so much, Rufus."

"You're welcome. I am going to go ahead and pay for the meal because I need to leave. I need to find the artist who designed these plates. The orange stripes next to abstract limes can only mean one thing."

"What does it mean?"

"I can't say because of confidentiality but if I don't find this guy in time there's going to be some terrible trouble with some people from his church."

"Ok, Rufus thanks so much. Can I give you one of my paintings sometime to thank you?"

"Sure, but nothing with a circus tent or rectangles. The elephant incident is none of my business."

Some of the names in this story have been changed

Sheila sat down at a meeting with the other social work interns and her supervisor at the elementary school where she was supposed to start doing at-risk counseling and play therapy.

"Good morning ladies," said Mr. G, her supervisor.

"Good morning," said a couple of the interns. There were four of them and they had been told that they would each start out working with five kids.

"You are all going to get your first case today. How do you feel about that?"

"Sounds good," said Sheila.

"I feel ready," said Ralphette, one of the other interns.

"Are we allowed to play a game with the kids?" asked Chi-chi, who was the only undergraduate student out of all of them.

"Yes, that is a great idea," said Mr. G. He handed out papers with kids' names and class numbers and the interns went to go get their kids out of class.

Sheila walked to a classroom to pick up Timmy, the kid who she had been assigned. He had been referred to the social work office because of some recent behavior problems and disrespect. He left class eagerly and on the way to the social work classroom Sheila said, "Timmy, would you like to play Connect Four?"

"Yeah," said Timmy. "I like that game."

Sheila had already gotten the game out of the closet, and they started playing as soon as they got to the room.

Sheila won the first game very easily.

"I'm a winner!" she shouted.

"Aww," said Timmy. "Can we play again?"

"Of course," said Sheila. "I plan to win multiple times."

They played again and Sheila won in just five moves. She used a trick she had taught herself when playing the game with her siblings years before.

"People think they can beat me at stuff," said Sheila. "But they can't. They can't beat me at social work. They can't beat me at Connect Four."

"I think I can beat you," said Timmy.

They played four more games and Sheila won all four times.

"Are we supposed to be talking about my problems?" asked Timmy.

"We don't have time to talk about problems, Timmy," said Sheila. "I can't really concentrate when people are yapping in my ear."

She won five more times and stood on the chair.

"Eleven to zero, losers, what do y'all think about that?"

The other interns and kids stared. Mr. G was not in the room.

A couple of the other kids laughed a little, but one girl looked scared.

"It's okay," said Friendlicia, the intern who was working with her. "It's okay, they're just playing a game." She was reaching for her cell phone.

"Who's next?" Sheila said to everyone, looking around. "I'm guessing that several of you can connect three, but I highly doubt that anyone is going to connect four today."

"I want to play!" said Tommy, a fourth grader who had been setting up some dominoes with Chi-chi. "Can I play?" he asked her.

"Uh, okay," Chi-chi said. The two kids got up to switch places. Tommy sat down at the Connect Four table and Timmy went to where Chi-chi was and started crying a little.

Sheila got down off the chair. "Ok, Mr........"

"Lastname."

"Mr. Lastname. You seem to think that you have a chance of lining up four checkers in my presence, and I'll be honest with you. It insults me that you are even trying."

Tommy nervously dropped a red checker into the blue Connect Four frame.

"Oh, going for the middle, huh? I know that trick." Sheila dropped a yellow checker next to the red checker.

They took turns and Sheila won quickly. She pulled the tab at the bottom of the Connect Four game and the checkers all scattered on the table.

"That's my favorite sound," she said. "Let me tell you something, Tommy. A lot of people come to school and sit in their desks and learn how to read. OK, we have those jokers at my school, too. But what matters? No, really, please tell me something that matters besides lining up four yellow checkers and then turning over all the tables?"

Sheila stood up so fast that her chair fell over and she then went over to a small table full of games, turned it over, and started kicking the mess of boards and pieces with her feet.

"No really, people, please tell me if there is anyone else who thinks they are going to take away my rightful inheritance?"

Friendlicia was on the phone, and Chi-chi and Ralphette were leading the kids out of the door. Some of the kids were reluctant to leave, all of them staring.

"I can beat you at Connect Four!" shouted one of them on his way out.

Sheila went to the games closet and started flinging games on the floor. She grabbed three Connect Four boxes and left the room, going into the classroom next door.

"Who's next?" she shouted. She started going around the room sliding the books off the kids' desks and setting up Connect Four games and dividing checkers.

Just then Mr. G and the security guard came in the room. He had Sheila's health card information with him.

"Sheila, you need to come downstairs with us," said Mr. G.

"I'm about to host a Connect Four tournament, Mr. G."

"You can host the tournament where you are going," he said.

"Oh are there some challengers who think they can beat me? Is it the same people who were able to keep the 3.0 GPA in social work school? I'll bet it is. Where are they?"

Mr. G and the security guard led Sheila out of the room while a few kids started to play Connect Four.

The Daughters of Jacob hospital was just down the street.

Sheila, Mr. G, and the security guard were greeted by a social worker at the hospital.

"We'll be right with you," said the social worker. "There is a big stack of games in the waiting area if you would like to work a puzzle or play checkers or something."

Slice of Life

"I thought of something funny one time," said Oatis.
"What was it? asked Rufus.
"I don't remember," said Oatis.
"Well do you want to go to Sheila's house?"
"Yeah."

They went to Sheila's house and she asked them to sit down for an orange. She gave them each a slice of orange on a silver plate. They ate their slices in silence until Sheila said "This orange is a special orange. It cost 99 cents at the grocery store."

"Wow, that is an expensive orange," said Rufus.

"Yeah, but obviously worth it," said Oatis. "My slice was delicious."

Rufus and Oatis left a few minutes later and talked about the visit on the way home.

"That was kind of weird," said Rufus. "I mean all she gave us was one orange slice."

"Mine was very yummy," said Oatis, "and I think I am going to become a missionary in China."

Extinction

Maybe the evangelicals didn't care enough about the black rhino but maybe it's a priority we would have gotten to if bad people didn't keep refusing to go to heaven.

Slimed

I was trying to pray up a special prayer for everyone in history who has ever taken goods to a market and then been ashamed in front of everyone like even in ancient times and I tried to think of some kind of gift basket for them or cheese plate or something and I finally thought you know what people might enjoy a collection of things like slime and silly putty and play-doh and floam like that might be a fun prize but then I thought that might make the situation worse because it's like hey guys y'all brought whatever necklaces and pottery to markets and had trouble and even these globs of goo sold better than that in our time.

Guinea Pig Extravaganza

What if you were doing pretty good in life but then started getting too many pet guinea pigs and then on Judgement Day most of your evaluation time was spent helping you understand that you weren't really supposed to have more than five guinea pigs at a time.

Poem

I did not say I was in charge of New York, guys.
I said I was good at writing and I am.
I was on the yearbook staff in high school
and I like cheesecake.

Roger

Some people don't think
you should call God a marshmallow
But all I mean is
He is understanding.

poem

Guys you really should not tell people
that you are Jesus Christ
unless you are mentally ill.

Poem

The fried peas
taste more like peas
than I remember
and I am wondering
if I did something bad.

Art Society

What if all the lawmakers were painters
and all the laws were about
how many people with blue shirts
could walk down the street at one time
or what kinds of cars should be parked
in front of which kinds of buildings.

poem

I don't know if it is good
for people with schizophrenia
to go to the mental hospital,
because what if when they are there
they see other people's hallucinations, too?

Guys some of y'all have some great shoes and some great hats too.

The people on the subway
probably are like
who died and made you the judge of all shoes?
But you know what guys?
Everyone dies,
or something like that.
Have you ever heard of Christianity?
It might do you some good.

Good news

Preachers preach their sermons
but in November at the gummy bear factory,
kids can trade acorns for candy.

Apple Jacks

People are going to be real sorry when I go to heaven
and it turns out that I like the same cereal as Jesus Christ.

Rats

In third grade I got in trouble
for chasing someone
and didn't get to go to the Christmas party
where they had showed the movie Rats of Nimh.

But now I live in New York
where there are millions of rats all around me
eating their lunch and peeking out of the sewers
and crawling around under the subways
as I get through each day.
they probably scamper over me as I sleep
so how about that for justice.

The next step is pet therapy for the New York Schools.

Poem: following a trail of dirty gummy bears

I followed a trail of dirty gummy bears and where did it lead?
Well it led to part of the sidewalk
where there were no more dirty gummy bears.

What does it mean?
I don't know.
I think it has something to do with snacks and walking.

5 poems from my trip to the hospital

1)
My roommate in the eeg unit is playing Candy Crush
and I am praying for all the hospitals
because I am too lazy to play Candy Crush
and I know everyone who's watching me on the eeg monitor
wants to get prayed for during a big jolt
where the eeg zig zags go crazy
and everyone gets zapped with my prayers
like when the Candy Crush speckled candy switches places with a striped one
and the whole board gets wiped out
like my memory from seizures.

2)
I like to go over to the window of my room in the epilepsy unit
and sit for a spell.

3)
Guys what if a monk
accidentally prayed a prayer
so powerful
that it pulverized a hospital.

4)
At the epilepsy unit they kept track of everything I did
 and disguised their vigilance as room service.
17 thousand dollars was a bargain.
People pay 40 dollars at museums
without seeing that kind of art.

5)
Guys I wonder if I could ever
accidentally electrocute someone
with one of my seizures.

Wilson's Five and Dime: Worth Every Penny

I am happy to be writing a business column for the *Revenant*. It seems fitting that my first column in this series should be about the jewel of South Carolina's business world, the centerpiece of all good commerce in the upstate, and the worldwide hub of all meaningful exchange: Wilson's Five and Dime.

Please do not tell me that you have not heard of Wilson's. That is really not a funny joke. Please do not tell me that you have only been to the Wilson's Five and Dime on Laurens Road in Greenville, because that is not funny, either. There are two more, you know: the Hudson Corners location and the beloved, miraculous, addictive, SPLIT LEVEL Berea Wilson's Five and Dime.

My love affair with Wilson's (which I admit has not always been chaste), began when I was about six or seven. I remember being in one of the toy aisles and knowing even then that this place was different. This store had squishy rubbery water thingies that other stores didn't have. This store had boxes and boxes of toys that other kids had to put quarters in machines for. This store had… you guessed it…. candy cigarettes.

Now, twenty-five years and 4809 boxes of candy cigarettes later, my love for Wilson's has done nothing but grow. It has grown and blossomed into an abiding, steady, passionate, and yes, violent, addiction. As a child, I liked going there for handbuzzers and rubber chickens. Now, as an adult, I tend to go there for, well, handbuzzers and rubber chickens.

Recently, I was able to acquire 144 bouncy balls from the Berea location. (People, it is worth the 45 minute drive from Taylors) I didn't even realize that I needed them until I saw the whole bag just sitting there on a table.

"Uh, just curious… how much would you charge for the whole bag?"

"$14.40."

For those of you who are used to buying things in pairs, or in six-packs, or in baker's dozens, 144 of anything is called a gross. I bought a gross of something. Yes, it was thrilling.

"You must be a teacher," the cashier said.

"Yes," I said. I was not lying. I really am a teacher, and I know that my eleventh grade American Lit students will be thrilled if I ever share any of the bouncy balls with them. Same with the Spongebob piñata and the forty-five pompom rings with googly eyes on them.

Googly eyes. I guess that's what I've spent the most money on at Wilson's Five and Dime. I don't know of a better investment than buying hundreds of plastic googly eyes to glue on stuff. Supergluing two googly eyes onto anything can transform it into a friendly little companion. Candy canes, peanuts, Christmas presents…. A pair of googly eyes could make a machine gun cute.

One of the great things about Wilson's is that even with all of the junk everywhere, the salespeople seem to know where everything is. If there is one little metal keychain that lights up with lasers, you can guarantee that any salesperson will be able to find it for you.

"Hey- five years ago, I bought a calculator watch for a dollar. Do you still have those?"

"Follow me."

Together, you weave through aisles bursting with boxes and racks of gizmos and whatchamacallits, and sure enough, right under the pirate hats, there's a little stack of calculator watches.

No, I am not making this up. I really did buy eight calculator watches for a dollar apiece. They have lasted me about five years. You wouldn't believe the compliments I get. I have, on occasion, just taken the watch off and said, "Here. It's yours." That is a luxury I have because the amazing deals I get at what is obviously the most cost-effective jewelry store in town. I suspect that Tiffany's is only managing to keep its head above water because Wilson's Five and Dime has not yet put its stores in the northern markets.

Really, not enough people think of Wilson's when it comes time to picking out a wardrobe. This should not be. Wilson's certainly has any accessory that would go with anything worth wearing, and sometimes they have complete costumes. I guarantee that half of the world's problems would be solved if people would just dress like pirates and princesses every now and then.

You probably think that Wilson's paid me to write this. Trust me. I am the one supporting Wilson's- not the other way around. Little by little, I have chosen to own a lot of stuff from Wilson's instead of owning a house. I have frittered away my money on trinkets and knick-knacks, and let me tell you- it's so worth it!!! Who wants food and shelter when you can have polka-dotted ribbons and glow-necklaces?

I have already politely asked God to build me a Wilson's Five and Dime to live in in heaven instead of a mansion. I am sure that people's living arrangements in heaven will be different during different millions of years. Sometimes, huge white mansions on rolling green hills will probably be cool. Other times, space stations might be en vogue. Me, I am going to just stick with a nice little run-down, perpetually stocked Wilson's Five and Dime at all times, and if it needs to float in space sometimes, hey- no problem. The zero gravity thing might be a problem in certain aisles, but I suspect that I will have plenty of duct tape to handle that situation.

For now, I must be content to shop there. It is true that they have a bunch of stuff that nobody needs, but whose fault is that? Not Wilson's. It is our duty, friends, to buy the gummy eyeballs and noisemakers first, and THEN find a need for them.

Where's The Cat?

Well, hello. This is my second column for the *Revenant*. I am going to try to introduce my topic gradually because it is a very controversial subject. It has to do with cats. It has to do with the presence and absence of cats. I will just tell you. In this column, I am posing a question that has baffled the local business community for years: How come Barnes and Noble doesn't have a cat?

Bookstores are supposed to have cats. Think about it. If you go into a book store, and you are trying to find a cookbook to give as a Christmas present, and you say to a bookseller, "Hi, where are your cookbooks?" wouldn't you be happier if the bookseller said "Over there near the cat."?

Or what if you were trying to decide between getting a book that you think you should read and getting a book that you actually want to read, and right then, a cat walks by. That would be so much better than if a cat didn't walk by.

Or what if you were at a bookstore and you ran into someone you knew, and they saw you buying a book about healing ringworm, and it ended up being an awkward situation. Wouldn't you feel better about the whole thing if at least there was a cat in the background?

You're probably thinking, "Which Barnes and Noble doesn't have a cat?" I will tell you. None of them. If you count the Spartanburg store, there are three Barnes and Noble bookstores in this area now, but no cats to be seen. And if you count the Asheville store and the other 600 stores in the country, that makes about 50 million Barnes and Nobles that don't have cats.

The newest Barnes and Noble in Greenville is actually located right in front of a PetSmart, but has anyone bothered to walk 300 yards and buy a cat? I'll give you a hint. No.

It gets even more ridiculous. The store manager at that Barnes and Noble used to work at PetSmart. If anyone could make a cat happen, she could. But has she? I'll give you a hint.

No. It actually gets worse. One of the managers of the PetSmart near Target used to be a Barnes and Noble Store manager. Has she taken care of this unfortunate situation? Let me help you guess. No.

With connections like these, you would think that every section of Barnes and Noble would have a cat in it. You would think that at the checkout counter, booksellers would be giving little kittens to anyone who buys a membership card. You would think that someone would have built a tunnel connecting PetSmart to Barnes and Noble so there would be enough cats for everyone to pet while they look at books and leave them on the floor for the workers to pick up.

The managers at these bookstores and pet stores are good at their jobs. They serve. They manage. They organize. They lead. Yet, somehow, they have failed to do their most important duty: putting cats where they need to be.

We can't just blame the managers, though. The problem is actually indicative of a much deeper societal problem. It has to do with frivolous lawsuits, government red tape, DHEC café regulations, mass apathy, allergies, and worst of all, fear.

There is really only one way that this problem will be solved. Customers must rise up and demand the cats that they deserve. Well, *deserve* is a strong word. The cats that they *want*. I am not saying that people need to picket Barnes and Noble, and I'm not saying that every letter to the Editor in every newspaper needs to be about the chain bookstore cat deficit. I am certainly not saying that people should resort to violence. I don't think that this is an "any means necessary" situation. But an onslaught of "Do y'all not have a cat?" comments during transactions might be a step in the right direction. Have I considered letting mice go in Barnes and Noble in order to attract cats? I will not lie. I have. I have given it a lot of consideration. But I promise that I have not done it. I am not promising that I won't.

There was a customer at the Haywood Road store who helped everyone out a few years ago by feeding some stray cats near the dumpster. It was much appreciated by the cats and by everyone who was relieved to at least have some cats NEAR the bookstore.

But should we, as humans, be satisfied with having cats *near* a bookstore? I do not think so. By the way, this column isn't really about cats at all. This is all a spiritual metaphor. Just kidding. It really is about cats and how Barnes and Noble should have some.

A Defense of Scripture Mints

My friend once posted an article on his blog where he warned skeptics of Christianity to stay away from Christian bookstores, suggesting that there is a cheap misrepresentation of Christianity being "sold" in those places. He criticized Christian bookstores for carrying merchandise that supposedly makes Christian faith seem foolish. He took special care to point out the so-called worthlessness of the trinkets and knick-knacks in the stores, in particular, things like "Scripture Mints," which are mints with Bible verses on the packaging, and "Testamints," which are mints with a cross carved in the middle. "Scripture candy," he wrote. "We can't forget the scripture candy."

Indeed we can't. If MacGyver can use a piece of gum and a battery to prevent a chemical explosion, just think what God could do with a "Testamint." I suspect that in God's hands, one little mint with a cross in the middle could potentially have more impact on this world than my entire life. Would God allow this? I don't know, but He could. God is clever and knows how to get bang for his buck.

In fact, not only could God use a testament to accomplish more than I ever could, He could do it even without using the Testamint for what it is designed for. The whole idea behind the gimmick (Yes, I'll admit it's a gimmick) is this: you keep the pack of Testamints in your pocket. Then, you offer one to someone, and seize the opportunity to tell them about Jesus. Will this ever work? Let's say, just for fun, that not one single Testamint accomplishes that goal. Let's say that in that regard, the whole endeavor is a total failure. Even then, I could show up on Judgement day and find out that I have been outdone by a Testamint. Consider the following possibilities:

-What if a person gives a Testamint to a child in church and the child ends up being quiet because of it, and the guy behind him, instead of being distracted by the child like he would have been, ends up hearing what the preacher says about diligence, and decides to do his best in school, and because of that, wins a scholarship to college, and then becomes involved in a night club scene where he gets so drunk one night that he flings his jacket out the window, and a homeless person finds the jacket and gets warm enough to live four more hours than he would have, and at the end of that four hours, mutters, "God help us," and God hears him and in response to that resemblance of a prayer, decides to postpone nuclear war for 25 years?

- What if a poet is hiking and decides to turn back because of fatigue, but finds a half-used pack of testaments in her backpack, and eats one (feeling guilty because the witness factor was wasted), but is refreshed enough to hike one more half-mile, where she comes across a mushroom that inspires her to write a poem that gets published in her high school literary magazine. And what if a fellow student reads the poem and decides that he would like to "get back to nature," and then tells his family, and they go hiking. And what if someone who works with his dad hears about it and decides to take his family hiking, and on that trip, he bonds with his son, who would have become a serial killer without the relationship with his dad that was cemented and invested in that weekend?

- What if, because someone eats a testament and still has the mint flavor in his mouth, he decides not to eat a whopper for lunch, but waits until later, where he just eats a salad, and because of that, salad-eating becomes a habit that adds four years to his life. And in those four years, he collects Hummel figurines, and his grandson inherits the collection, and eventually gives one of the figurines to a neighbor, who places it on her coffee table. And then that lady's daughter "borrows" the Hummel character and plays Barbies with it, and while playing Barbies with it, she and her sister imagine a scenario where the Hummel comes to visit Barbie and Barbie is out of the Hummel's favorite soup, so Barbie gets in the toy convertible, goes to the Fisher Price grocery store, buys the Hummel's favorite soup, and makes the Hummel feel at home. Well, say that the older sister makes such an impression on her younger sister during this little Barbie session that 30 years later, her younger sister fixes a guest his favorite type of soup, and he is so overwhelmed by her hospitality that he marries her, and 16 generations later, a descendant puts a library in a retirement home as an Eagle Scout project. Well, it might be a small library, but what if one of the books in it was H.G.Well's <u>The Time Machine</u>, and a guy at the home recommends the book to his grandson, who, 40 years later, sees someone on the bus reading that book and strikes up a conversation about it? Well, say that the girl sitting in front of them overhears the conversation and decides to build a time machine. She fails. But her efforts are mentioned in the presence of a fourth grade teacher who mentions it in class, saying that time travel is impossible because of certain paradoxes. Well, one student may take that as a personal challenge and could end up spending his life inventing a time machine. Well, say a lady travels back in time and gets stuck in the middle east about three thousand years ago. And say she starts a family there, and one of her descendants is on the board of city people who make decisions about roads. And someone says, "hey. Let's have a cobblestone road in Jerusalem." And she says, "No, keep it dirt." And they deliberate for hours. Then, one day, a blind guy is sitting near the road and Jesus sees him and spits on the ground, making mud, and uses it to heal the blind man. And then hundreds of years later, a person is invited to a church where the preacher talks about the Pharisee's bad reaction to Jesus healing that blind man. Because of that sermon, this guy decides to try to be genuine instead of being a fraud. Because he is sincere, his neighbor decides to invite him for supper. He takes his family over to his neighbor's house, and they have bread with butter on it. Well, his son likes the butter, and wants his family to be able to afford butter, so he gets a job carrying wood. Well, one day his friend comes over and carves a pipe out of the wood. He is so proud of his creation that he makes more, and eventually makes pipes for a living.

Woodworking skills are passed down through several generations, and one day a descendant starts making violins. He sells one to a lady who gives it to her child, but it is stolen at school. But it ends up in the hands of a little boy who plays it in the market square in front of an artist who is so charmed by the delightful fiddler that he creates a Hummel figurine of a boy playing a violin. The Hummel ends up being put in a shop window, where it is discovered by a guy who started collecting Hummels during the last four years of his life....

    I am certain that I will be outdone by every single Testamint after all is said and done, but that is fine with me as long as I do what I am supposed to. If Jesus can use mud to heal a blind man, he can use cheap, gimmicky candy to heal a blinder man. Skeptics, flee to the Christian specialty shops! Buy some Testamints! Taste and see that the Lord is good.

Impaired Judgment Day

I recently wrote a little poem that said "Of course I'm scared about Judgement Day. You would be, too if you had laughed at someone in a wheelchair because they looked like an elephant." I think it's a pretty funny poem, and it is all true, of course, but I am kind of scared about sharing it with a lot of people, because what if I get in trouble on Judgement Day for writing a poem like that?

I wrote another poem about Judgement Day called "So What If I Get A Plastic Fork On Judgement Day?" It is a poem about how what if instead of getting awesome rewards on Judgement Day, Jesus just gives me a plastic fork in front of everyone, and I go back to my seat, and it is awkward for everyone, and everyone feels sorry for me for millions of years, but I am thankful for my plastic fork and use it to eat every meal, and then one day, millions of years after Judgement Day, I find out that the fork is a key to a whole new world full of googly-eyed creatures and it has a snack bar with plastic forks that are also keys to new worlds. It was also a pretty funny poem, and at the same time, my real thoughts.

I also wrote yet another poem about Judgement Day a few years ago, called "Performance Review Phrases I Don't Want To Hear On Judgement Day." It was a list of job evaluation phrases that I truly don't want to hear on Judgement Day, such as "Despite coaching and training, Sarah's productivity remained low," and "Sarah hesitated to work with leadership to meet goals." The last one listed was "Sarah ate with her mouth open." It was pretty funny.

And guess what? Those aren't even all of my Judgement Day poems. It's not all I write about or anything, but a few weeks ago, after writing several Judgement Day poems in a row, I realized that it is a frequent topic of mine, and I wondered if there was a reason for it. At first, the reason seemed obvious—it could be because I am crazy. It's because of my manic depression, etc. (the "etc" part is pretty serious. Let's not talk about it.) I'm mentally ill, and talking about Judgement Day too much is what mentally ill people do. It's what we're here for. In his book, *I Know This Much Is True*, Wally Lamb tells the story of a guy whose twin brother has schizophrenia. One of the opening scenes of the book is the narrator's memory of being with his brother at a restaurant called "Friendly's." The narrator describes what happened:

Our waitress approached—a high school kid wearing two buttons:'Hi, I'm Kristin,' and 'Patience, please. I'm a trainee.' She asked us if we wanted to start out with some cheese sticks and a bowl of soup.

"You can't worship both God and money, Kristin," Thomas told her. America's going to vomit up its own blood."

Just like I am not sure if I am supposed to write poems about laughing at people in wheelchairs who look like elephants, I am not sure if I am really supposed to find that scene funny, but I do. I find it hilarious, and when I read those few pages in a library years ago, I immediately checked out the book and read all 800 something pages as fast as I could. It was an effective scene, and part of that reason is because some people with certain kinds of mental illness really do say that kind of stuff all the time. People say it on street corners, in homeless shelters, in mental hospitals, and sadly, especially with today's problematic mental health care situation, in jails. (The jail problems are tragic. America, you're going to vomit up your own blood.)

Often, our kinds of religious ramblings and rants are dismissed as crazy talk, and we are sedated with antipsychotics until we stop saying it, or at least say it more quietly in our sleep.

But I figured out that at least with my own obsession about Judgement Day, whether I am freaking out about my own future Judgement Day experience or that of the people I care about, which really sometimes is everyone, there are reasons for that, and misfiring synapses are only some of those reasons. There is a complex network of thoughts, feelings, experiences, and illness that have affected my relgious beliefs, and, let's face it—problems, and I think that examining these factors is interesting and contains important implications regarding the experience of others who exhibit obvious religion problems, or, maybe, religious beliefs that only appear to be fully problematic.

Let's start with some background information. It is important for you to know that I had twelve years of perfect attendance in school. I did not miss a day of school from first grade through twelfth grade. I tell you that for two reasons: first, to brag, because come on, that is really awesome, isn't it? I should get something for that, like free candy on Judgement Day or something. Secondly, I tell you that, because I think it is an indication of how important achievement is to me. When I was in first grade, I got a certificate for one year of perfect attendance, and at that awards assembly, I saw someone get a trophy for three years of perfect attendance and decided then that I would try for the three year trophy. Sure enough, I earned that trophy, and then, the five year plaque, and with the help of my family, kept on going all the way through being at school on senior skip day in high school, eventually showing up to school every day for twelve years. Yes, there were some tardies, and I remember freaking out in fourth grade about possibly being late after attending a prayer breakfast at my family's Presbyterian church. But on time or late, I showed up to school every day and got some certificates along the way. All mental illness aside, it kind of makes sense that if I care that much about awards days, J a day like Judgement Day is going to matter a lot.

There is more background stuff that might be even more important. It is important for you to know that I believed what they told me at church. They told me that Jesus died for our sins, and I believed it. They told me that others needed to know this, and I believed it. They told me that obeying God was important and that serving others and obeying God was a good way for us to help others find out all the important stuff we knew. I am grateful they told me this, and I am grateful for the blessings and experiences I have had because of it. Even with its inevitable difficulties, the Christian lifestyle is a blessing and a privilege.

    I felt this gratitude when I went off to college, and was thankful for all aspects of my upbringing and was eager to share my life and faith with others, even as I started experiencing weariness, growing anxiety, and rapidly worsening insecurity. My freshman and sophomore years of college, I took as many classes as I could, leaning towards choices that prompted creative output, I participated in a variety of extra curricular activities, and I signed up for volunteer work that appealed to me, including helping out with an organization that provided camp experiences for kids with AIDS and a Christian ministry for high school kids called Young Life.

    These responsibilities became increasingly difficult and burdensome to me, and I started to become so shy that interaction with others, especially strangers, was almost unbearable. I started having trouble sleeping, and I often felt like crying. I couldn't concentrate enough to read, and had trouble finding energy to do basic tasks. One time I realized that it had taken me several minutes to tie my shoe, and another time I had to crawl to the shower because I was so exhausted. My Christmas job at Toys R Us was the ten ton truckload of haybales that broke the camel's back, and by Christmas, I was suicidal. One night when I couldn't sleep, I staggered out of bed and sat on my floor in front of my bookshelf, begging God to annihalate me. I knew from church that this was not a possibility, and that souls are eternal, whether they go to heaven or to hell. I lay on the floor and was certain that I was being sucked into hell that very moment. It was just like they had described on the mission trip I went on after junior year of high school. It was agony and loneliness with no hope. I wondered if God wanted me to go to hell and was asking me to go there out of obedience, so I tried to psychologically go further. What I did didn't feel good, but I could tell that it didn't work, either. I also remember trying to extinguish myself on purpose, thinking if I willed myself so far into hell that I might eventually go away forever, but it didn't work either. Thinking that I had to be pretty far down there, I tried to find a friend, whispering first to Judas, one of Jesus's disciples who I thought might be in hell and might be willing to be my friend, and when he didn't answer, I wondered if Satan was there and might want to be my friend, remembering that he himself was originally one of God's creations and must surely have some remnant of friendworthy substance in his being. I did not sense any sort of response from anyone. I also remember worrying that I might be the Anti-Christ, and I tried to make myself be willing to do that if that's what God wanted me to do, but feeling too ashamed, inadequate, and unworthy even to be used in that manner. After staying on the floor a little while trying to cry but unable to find any relief through tears, I looked up, saw the books on my shelf, and figured that I must still be on earth. I staggered back up to my bed and kept on living.

So that is pretty sad, isn't it. Well guess what-- I got over it. I read some fairy tales, I finished working at Toys R Us, I read *Atlas Shrugged*, which said not to be lazy, and I went back to school and graduated. I graduated and got some certificates, which, I will remind you, are very important to me.

Before I graduated, I did go missing in New York City for a few days, but I turned up in a hospital with just a bad case of manic depression. Despite the multi-state news coverage, it wasn't a big deal, and it wasn't a big deal after I moved back in with my parents and then turned up in another mental hospital in Georgia. Or when I got sent to the next mental hospital in Greenville, SC a year and a half later. The food there was great, and every time I get sent to the other hospital in Greenville I think about how if only that first hospital took my insurance, I could have that broccoli and cheese casserole I like so much almost anytime I want. But the hospital I usually go to has a salad bar, so that is nice, too.

There are some intersesting hospital stories from my manic episodes, and there are interesting things to say about life in between. But let's concentrate on the important thing, which is Judgement Day.

First, let's define Judgement Day. Guess what? I can't. I am just not sure what it is. I know that it has something to do with all of our hearts, actions, and deeds being exposed before an all knowing (and thankfully) loving God, and maybe before all of humanity, and I imagine it happening right after I die, though I don't know if that is really true. And there are places in the Bible where Jesus himself says that we will give an account for every idle word, but there are also places where it says that our sins are as far away as the east is from the west. And from what I have gathered from different sermons and Bible reading and my own speculation, there is disagreement about whether it is a one-day event or whether it might be a more gradual, non-"awards day" type of reckoning. People also disagree about whether it only has to do with people being sent to either heaven or hell, or whether it has to do with distribution of rewards, and many pastors can't even explain the relationships between all that. I have also wavered between Protestant, Orthodox, and Catholic views of these topics, and still don't have it settled in my mind. I don't even want to try to define and distinguish between the differences for fear that I would misrepresent everyone and have to answer for it on Judgement Day.It is still quite a mystery to me now, even after thinking about it almost constantly for years, but for some of those years, it was not just an interesting mystery, but a terrifying unknown- a constant threat of unbearable shame and grief, and a constant source of despair.

Either right after my first hospitalization or right after graduation, my parents took me to a psychiatrist and I was put on medicine: first, for many months, Lithium and Risperdal, and eventually Depakote and Risperdal. After suffering immediately from psychotic manic episodes upon each attempt to go off risperdal, an antipsychotic that is usually only used temporarily to treat mania in patients with manic depression, it became clear that I would need to be on it all the time, and probably for the rest of my life. "The rest of my life" sounds like a long time, but that's not necessarily the case when you are suicidal, which I was by the summer after graduation from college. I had no idea that my medicines were causing much of my suffering, but they were. I felt like being in bed all the time, but I couldn't sleep. I was thirsty and started drinking at least a pitcher of Kool-Aid per day, and I felt hopeless about the future. I had been planning to try to get an advertising job in New York City, since advertising was my college major and a childhood dream, but did not feel confident about the job search and was aware of my parents' legitimate fears about letting me go to a city like that while experiencing such instability. In October of 1999, I started working at our local Barnes and Noble. I started in the music department. The shifts were eight and a half hours long, and I could barely stand the loneliness and boredom. Music sellers at Barnes and Noble are often the only employees in the music department for hours at a time. It is also a job that requires standing all day long. Thousands of people work jobs like this, and some people in some countries are on their feet for fourteen hour days. So let's not complain too much, but let's not pretend that it was a candy and award extravaganza, either. Eight hours felt like a lot to me, and it was quite an adjustment. All day, I would stare at the emergency exit in the back of the building and imagine myself running out of it. I couldn't wait to get an advertising job so I could say something funny on the intercom and then walk out that door on my last day. The boredom and loneliness was worsened by my exhaustion, lethargy, and drowsiness. I had no idea whether it was the illness or the medicine. I just knew that manic depressives were never supposed to stop taking their medicine, so I took mine every day.

The most difficult thing about work was my intense social anxiety. It was worse than it ever had been, even during my first major depression in college, and I could barely look at people enough to help them at the cash register. I was constantly filled with dread, and I felt filled with fear every time a customer came in the music department.

I wanted to kill myself. I had not had real sleep in months, and I felt constant shame, even when I was alone and lying in bed, which is all I did when I wasn't at work. I started daydreaming, and I couldn't stop. I wasn't imagining myself doing things, but instead I created characters and imagined them living life. I felt that I was too horrible and despicable to even put in my own daydream (or should I say nightmare). I made one cameo appearance in the daydream, and that was when one of the characters had a piece of art I made on their wall. Other than that, it was totally an escape from my life. The plot changed all the time, and I repeated scenes in my mind, like a soap opera. Some might say that this is normal, and that is why such thing as real soap operas exist. For me, it was not normal. I was not used to using my mind like this, and I couldn't stop. Though it gave me some relief from the boredom and pain, it also intensified the guilt and shame I was already experiencing, because I knew it was different than the real creative process of thinking up a story. I knew it was some kind of fantasy, and I knew that it wasn't good. Oddly, one of the main things that happened in it was that my characters won lots of awards all the time. They won like every award you could ever win, and they always did so despite horrible circumstances. I do have them beat on one thing, though, and that is perfect attendance. They did not get perfect attendance awards.

Later, I would find out that my medicine problems were a big part of why I couldn't stop daydreaming. I don't know if it was partially my body's attempt to get the sleep that it had not had in months and eventually years, or if the medicine itself triggered certain brain activity, but after years of struggle and shame and an important medicine change, I was able to fight off the habit by praying and reading instead, and I, at least for now, have relief from the horrible addiction that gave such false relief.

The daydream problem was just one factor in this set of circumstances that led to constant fear about Judgement Day. At the time, I really didn't necessarily think of it as "Judgement Day." I was just very suicidal and very aware that on any day, I could give up, kill myself, and forfeit a lifetime's reward in heaven, not to mention causing my family a lifetime of grief. I did not know how much longer I would last, so I was faced with the possibility of facing God and multitudes of scrutinizing human onlookers on any day in the near future. There was another problem that increased my anxiety, and that was the feeling that everyone in heaven was already reading my mind and watching me. I mean, what else would they be doing? Playing harps? I don't think so. No, they were watching my daydream on a screen, and as soon as my strength ran out and I killed myself, I would be in front of them and have to watch them watch that video and videos of all my sins on a screen. It really was not something I was looking forward to, and one hope that I might have ordinarily had, which was that maybe Jesus really did die for our sins and there wouldn't be hell to pay, was also in question, because my state of mind did not seem to be characteristic of someone who had what many Christians would call "saving faith." I did not realize it at the time, but some aspects of my illness make certainty about anything almost unattainable for me, so even trust in God and certainty that He had already guaranteed prevention of Judgement Day horrors was probably not something I was even capable of feeling and experiencing.

It's quite a predicament to be in, really, and there were a few more stressors mixed in as well. For one thing, my anxiety and depression made every interaction with bookstore customers be a source of suffering, and I often felt anger towards people. I felt like telling people to go to hell sometimes, but according to my parents, because of my pre-existing condition, if I lost my medical insurance, I could never be insured for manic depression again. I don't know if that was really true, or if there were laws that changed that along the way, but it is stressful to have urges to lash out at people, hundreds of opportunities a day to do so, and the knowledge that one mistake could cost you your job and insurance and put you in permanent debt for the rest of your life. Manic Depression is expensive. And I really felt that permanent debt might also cause many people harm, including myself on Judgement Day.

Then, the terrorists destroyed the two towers in NYC and killed all those people, and of course I thought it was my fault. How could it not be?

Please, if you are feeling sorry for me, try to feel even sorrier, because there is more. If you are not feeling sorry for me, why not? Is it because I got to work in a nice bookstore that smells like coffee and cookies? You have a good point. But did you know that I had to alphabetize? Well guess what? I did. After about a year and a half, I started working in the book part of the store, and I often had to alphabetize. And guess what else? I wasn't good at it. I tried to give myself more reasons to put books in the right places, like saying "God, please give everyone in Africa 45 million blessings for each book I put back in the right place," but it just increased the guilt when I was too tired to alphabetize efficiently. It really did give me a constant feeling of failure, and do you know what that does to someone who is facing the possibility of Judgement Day any day? I will tell you what it does. It makes them want to kill themselves. And do you know what that does? It makes them worry about Judgement Day. And do you know that that does? It makes them want to kill themselves. And do you know what that does? It makes them think about pink ponies. Just joking. It makes them worry about Judgement Day.

It is true that I found some relief, but most of my relief also caused more guilt. The daydreaming, the fast food, drinking entire pitchers of Kool-Aid, driving around in my car wasting gas, and laying in bed for fifteen hours a day were my main forms of relief, and I felt guilty all the time about all of it. Add that guilt to the guilt I had about selling some of the embarrassing and objectionable merchandise at Barnes and Noble, and that's a lot of guilt and shame for a person to bear with no hope of finding relief, except to die, which would most certainly just magnify my shame and multiply the onlookers. The anguish lasted for at least three or four years, finally with some long term relief from the medicine change and with the start of grad school, a glorious and beautiful ray of hope and source of intellectual nourishment.

I think those experiences are part of why I think and write about Judgement Day so much. You're probably still thinking about those coffee and cookie smells and thinking I had it pretty good. Well guess what? I know I had it pretty good. I'm not stupid. I know a blessing when I see one. I kept working at Barnes and Noble for twelve years, and I was thankful to be there. The fact is that the place does sometimes smell like cookies, and the friendships I had there are to die for, or really, in my case, to live for. My coworkers, bosses, and even some customers sustained me with jokes, compliments, and attention, and I hope I get to see them get their reward on Judgement Day, though the whole idea of it also terrifies me.

Some of my fears have subsided. I have more faith in God and His mercy, and I feel more certain that whatever Jesus did on that cross really does excuse me from condemnation and alienation from God. Most of my concerns now are for other people on Judgement Day.

I don't know if other mentally ill people with religion problems have histories like mine. I can only speculate about how their upbringing, heartbreaks, and medical situations factor in to the beliefs that they mumble and ramble about. But I suspect that there is more to the story than just symptoms of illness, and I hope that like me, they see some advantages to their suffering. In a way, my long term anguish and stand-off with the gates of hell is something I wouldn't wish on my worst enemy, but in a way, I think it is the exact type of mercy that some people need in order to realize what's at stake in this life and in the next. Close calls with hell or earthly reminders of it can inspire repentance and drive people towards a faith and life that will provide them with glory, hope, and relief on what must be one of the most important events in all of human existence: the time, whenever and however that may be, when everyone reaps what they sow, and people get what they deserve, and in some mysterious way through Christ, also get spared what they deserve. Sometimes I am tempted to dismiss my own beliefs and experiences as the rantings and ravings of a lunatic, but I am certain that there are much worse religion problems a person can have, like facing God on Judgement Day after rejecting His mercy.

Ancient Chinese Moon Poems

I was happy to get to read some poems from ancient China because I actually think about ancient China from time to time. I think about ancient China and regular China, and it is almost always in the same situation. It is when I am walking to my car at night in the back parking lot of the Barnes and Noble where I work. What usually happens is that I see the moon, and think about how it is the same moon that goes over China, and sometimes I think about how God is up there, too, and how He was also watching over the people from ancient China, and if you take into account His being eternal and transcending time, in a way, He is still watching over them right now. I don't think those thoughts every time I go to my car, and not even every time I look at the moon. I am not sure why it is usually China that I think of, though it is probably because I like China and because it is so foreign and far away. It is just, for some reason, a recurring set of thoughts that I have thought from time to time. When I think of ancient China, I don't think of a particular century or anything. I just think of a quiet night scene near some pagodas like the scenes I have seen in movies.

So I was excited to read the poetry in *Mountain Home, The Wilderness Poetry of Ancient China*, translated by David Hinton, and very happy to see that it was mostly about nature, because this really matched some of my perceptions, as limited as they are, about that time and place. And then, when I saw that in addition to poems about rivers and mountains, there were lots of poems that featured the moon, I was even happier, and wondered if the people in ancient China looked at the moon and thought of me. I am kind of joking about hoping they thought of me, because how could they even imagine cars and parking lots and Barnes and Nobles, but I did think it was possible that they might have thought about the moon and wondered about other people in far away places and times under that same moon.

Well, it kind of seems like they mostly didn't. It really seems like they were more interested in the moments they were experiencing with the moon right there, and they just wanted to capture the beauty of the immediate scenes right then. Which is fine. I am not mad at them or anything, and their poetry is still very beautiful. This is a nice line: "Moonrise startles mountain birds,:/here and there, cries in a spring gorge." That's fine just as it is. Don't worry about me, Meng Hao-jan. I get plenty of attention and don't need you to think of me when you are in the rickshaw lot behind the paper-making hut near the Han river.

Really, I am just happy to think of all those Chinese poets as being under the same moon as me, and I am glad they wrote stuff down about it, because until now, that's way more than I have done. And several of these poets, in addition to describing the moon in a nature scene, provided more of a look at life back then in their moon scenes, which helps me picture ancient China more easily. Mei Yao-ch'en does this, and in one of his poems, "Lunar Eclipse," unlike most of the other ancient Chinese poetry, there is even some indication that he was, in fact, wondering how things were going for me at Barnes and Noble. Like many of his poems, the poem goes into more detail about daily life and human interactions than those of some of the other ancient Chinese poets. This particular poem starts off with a description of a maid running in to the house and talking about "things beyond belief," and then the moon images are introduced: "about the sky all turned to blue glass,/ the moon to a crystal of black quartz./ It rose a full ten parts round tonight,/ but now it's just a bare sliver of light." Then, it's back to the humans: "My wife hurries off to fry roundcakes, and my son starts banging on mirrors:/ it's awfully shallow thinking, I know,/ but that urge to restore is beautiful." And here, finally: "The night deepens. The moon emerges,/ then goes on shepherding stars west." Now I know that by "west," he is not necessarily officially talking about modern Western Civilization, but really just talking about the direction that the moon is going in, but if you take into account the fact that if the moon keeps on going "west," which it did, then it would rotate around the world thousands of times, which it did, eventually stopping by the Barnes and Noble parking lot in South Carolina. So I guess what I am saying is that really, maybe some of these people did care about us, and I am flattered to be included in such a nice moon poem.

Despite the way most of these poets concentrate on moments and the immediate setting around them, there actually are somewhat frequent references to the moon as being a symbol of permanence. Rivers and mountains are also more permanent aspects of nature, compared to say, clouds, trees, or "wheat blossoms that turn to snow" in moonlight. (p.164) Every now and then, in these poems, there will be an acknowledgement of nature outlasting the admiring humans. This is expressed in poet Tu Fu's famous lines, "The nations fall into ruins; rivers and mountains continue." (p. 96) Po Chu-i also had some poems that expressed sentiments like this. One is his poem "In The Mountains, Asking The Moon."

It's the same Ch'amg-an moon when I ask
Which doctrine remains with us always.

It flew with me when I fled those streets,
And now shines clear in these mountains,

Carrying me through autumn desolations,
Waiting as I sleep away long slow nights.

If I return to my homeland some day,
It will welcome me like family. And here,

It's a friend for strolling beneath pines
Or sitting together on canyon ridgetops.

A thousand cliffs, ten thousand canyons—
It's with me everywhere, abiding always.

This is the type of permanence I associate with the moon, and though ultimately, I believe human souls may outlast even the most long-lasting aspects of our surroundings, including the earth and moon, which may only be around for billions of years, I do think that in this lifetime, it does make sense to remember that the moon has outlasted the earthly lifespans of billions of people, making it a perfect symbol of endurance and permanence. To see this recognized by someone from hundreds of years ago, and especially seeing how he even regarded the moon as a steady and constant companion, reinforces my own appreciation of the moon. Another poet, Wei Ying-Wu, also has a poem in which he refers to the moon as a companion, and he describes the moon's "boundless light,/ all silver-pure azure leading us to perfection." It is a beautiful description of something that has been a source of inspiration and beauty for people from all cultures and times, and reading these kinds of poems makes me kind of understand why Li Po, a Chinese poet from the 700s, would die trying to hug the moon's reflection.

Work Cited

Hinton, David. *Mountain Home: the Wilderness Poetry of Ancient China*. New York, NY: New Directions Pub., 200

Recipes from a cookbook I am working on:

Potato Casserole

    First, go to the grocery store. Get a bag of frozen shoestring potatoes. Try to get Ore Ida if you can. Then go get a big container of sour cream. Don't get lite sour cream. It will ruin the meal and your life. Then, go get a can of cream of chicken soup. Don't get low fat or healthy choice. Again, you don't want a ruined life. I also recommend getting Campbells, because the high sodium will offset the sodium depletion caused by your psychiatric medicine.
    Ok, then, when you are getting the soup, you need to realize that while you were in the dairy section, you should have gotten a pack of cheese. So go back and get a 2-cup bag of finely shredded mild cheddar cheese.
    At this point, realize that you probably should have gotten a grocery cart.
    Pay for your groceries, go home, mix it all together and bake at 400 degrees for 45 minutes or more. It is kind of nice to sprinkle extra cheese on top.

Corn Casserole

Mix up a can of drained corn, a can of creamed corn, a cup of sour cream, an egg, some melted butter (however much you want), and a box of Jiffy corn muffin mix. Dump it all into a casserole dish and bake at 350 for 30-40 minutes. You can sprinkle cheese on top and bake it for five more minutes if you want to be a show-off who everyone resents.

Cheesy Chicken Enchiladas

Buy some tortillas and reflect on the tragic immigration problems. Pray a little and wallow in your despair.

Then get some cream of chicken soup, a pack of shredded cheese, a big container of sour cream, and a pack of chicken. By the time you check out, you will probably have forgotten about the immigration problems.

Go home and cook the chicken. You can boil it, or you can sautee it in a frying pan. Just do whatever you want. Why are you asking me to make all of your decisions for you?

Ok, now, shred the chicken, and in a big bowl, mix it with a can of cream of chicken soup, most of the cheese, and lots of sour cream. Scoop some of the mixture onto tortillas, roll them up, put them all side by side in a casserole dish, cover with cheese, and bake for 20 minutes. Then eat. Try to ignore the tormenting immigration worries that surface as you eat the enchiladas.

Hint- if you don't feel like cooking chicken, then get one of those rotisserie chickens and shred it up.

Chicken and Rice Casserole

This recipe is similar to the enchilada recipe. That is because I pretty much copied that recipe. Ok, cook some chopped chicken in a frying pan with mustard powder and worschestire sauce. Cook some rice (1-2 cups pre-cooked) Mix some cream of chicken soup with a bunch of sour cream. Mix the chicken, rice, goop, and a whole bunch of shredded cheese together and put in a casserole dish. A square one might be good. Save some of the sour cream goop to make a layer on top of the other stuff, and then sprinkle cheese on top of that. It is kind of good to add crumbled bacon (already cooked) among the cheese. Bake at 350 for twenty minutes. Then eat in secret by yourself.

Sausage Pinwheels

This is a great breakfast food. It is basically cheese and sausage rolled up in a rectangular crescent roll dough and then chopped into pinwheels and then cooked at 350 degrees for about 10 minutes or less or more.

Ok, you will need two packs of Pillsbury crescent rolls, some sausage (the kind that's crumbly when it's cooked), and a whole bunch of grated cheese. How much cheese, you ask? I don't know. What, do you think I spend all my time just measuring cheese? Well, I don't.

Ok, anyway, get your mom to cook the sausage, because who wants to spend all their time cooking sausage? I don't.

Once she cooks the sausage, unroll crescent dough but instead of separating the perforated triangles, keep pairs of triangles together to make rectangles. Spread crumbled sausage and cheese over each rectangle, roll it up, maybe refrigerate it, and then slice and bake. This is great to bake in the morning so you can serve it warm. It might be smart to cook the sausage and roll up the rolls the night before, because who wants to get up at 6 a.m. to cook sausage? I sure don't.

French Bread Pizza

Just make a French bread pizza. This really shouldn't need any explanation. You cut a loaf of French bread in half, and then slice the halves in half and spread some sauce, cheese, and toppings on it. It's really not that complicated, and very multicultural.

Lemon Whippersnappers

Okay, get some lemon cake mix and a thing of cool whip. Make sure you have an egg somewhere, preferably in the refrigerator, because it wouldn't be safe to use an egg from last Easter. Get some powdered sugar. And some taco seasoning. Just joking about the taco seasoning. Why would you put taco seasoning in lemon cookies? Try not to be so gullible. There are a lot of tricksters in this world and you don't want to be fooled into putting taco seasoning in lemon cookies.

Okay, anyway, mix together the cake mix, one egg, and cool whip. This makes the dough. Then put some powdered sugar in a bowl, cover your fingers with it, and grab small globs of the dough to roll around in the powdered sugar. Put the globs of dough on a cookie sheet. Bake at 350 degrees for 8-10 minutes. Then take cookies out. Put them on a cooling rack if you want, or just wait for them to cool on the pan. It's not really that big of a deal either way. Listen, you don't have time to be obsessing over whether to use a cooling rack. Like I said before, there are tricksters out there, and they are plotting to harm you. They want you to take the cookies out of the oven too soon so they're too gooey, or too late, so they are too stiff. They want you to take the cookies to a party and accidentally drop them. You know those other people at the grocery store who are also in the baking aisle when you are there? Those are the people I am talking about. They are trying to beat you at cooking. They want people to like their food better, but don't let them win, okay? Just keep making the best lemon whippersnappers you can.

Bacon Tomato and Goat Cheese Sandwich

The concept of this sandwich is very simple. You're basically going to make a sandwich out of tomato slices, crispy strips of bacon, and globs of goat cheese. It's best on white bread with mayonnaise. That's all. That's the recipe. It's a sandwich.

Fudge

I'm not going to lie. This is a difficult recipe. You will need to melt a stick and a half of butter and add three cups of sugar and 5 ounces of evaporated milk. That's already so much work that you might feel like giving up. But don't give up, okay, because this fudge is really yummy. Keep stirring it at medium heat, okay. You can taste it a little if you want to. Turn the heat up to medium high and bring it to a rolling boil. Basically this means that bubbles form and it seems kind of boiling. Okay, this is the complicated part. I am getting kind of discouraged, aren't you? But we have to keep going because this fudge is so yummy. Okay. When it starts to boil, set a timer for exactly five minutes. Don't mess this up. It has to be five minutes.

Okay, at the end of the five minutes, remove the mixture from the heat, and dump in 12 ounces of chocolate chips. Stir it all until all the chips are melted in and it is starting to look kind of like liquid fudge. Your hand is tired, isn't it? Well I warned you that this wasn't an easy recipe. Let's not give up, though. It might help to whisper "I'm not giving up until I have made some fudge." Now add one jar of marshmallow puff. The jar of marshmallow puff might have a recipe for fudge on it, but if you use that recipe, you won't get all the coaching I am giving you, which is important, isn't it, because this is not easy, is it? It's okay to say that. Alright, we are almost there. Are you okay? It is okay to cry a little if you need to. Stir the marshmallow puff until the mixture looks smooth and fudgy, and then, if you want to, add a half cup or more of chopped pecans. Then, dump the mixture into a 9 by 13 pan. Smooth it all out and let it sit for a few hours. Guess what? You just made fudge!!!! Slice it with a knife-- maybe just a table knife so you don't ruin your pan. You just made fudge! You just made fudge!! I am so happy for you. I knew you could do it.

Forgotten Cookies

This recipe only has four ingredients, but it might take some practice to get it just right. All you need is egg whites, sugar, chocolate chips, and a little bit of vanilla. I sometimes forget the vanilla, but that is not why they are forgotten cookies. They are called forgotten cookies because after you make the goop and spoon it on to tin foil covered pans, you put them in the oven for several hours and "forget about them."

First, preheat the oven to 350 degrees. You can experiment with different temperatures if you want. You will turn off the oven as soon as you put the cookies in. I am telling you this now and will tell you again at the end of the recipe so you don't forget.

Okay, here is how to make the goop. The hard part is separating the eggs. You take two whites, which means breaking the egg in half and pouring the yolk back and forth into the shells until all the white comes off from around it and goes into the bowl. You can save the yolks and make hollandaise sauce for some ham or vegetables or eggs benedict or something if you want. But anyway this forgotten cookie recipe is a great recipe to double, but the standard recipe calls for two egg whites. Okay, now, you have to beat the egg whites with a mixer until they are stiff and white and form peaks if you lift the beater. Now, beat in a half cup of sugar, maybe even ¾ cup. And add a little capful of vanilla. Some people measure the vanilla, and that is good for them. I don't measure it. I think that it is enough to just remember it in the first place.

There is one last thing to add to the goop, and that is chocolate chips. Just add however many you want. Mix it up, spoon onto the pan, (don't forget the tin foil), put them in the oven, TURN THE OVEN OFF!, and then try to find something else to do while you wait for the cookies.

Before you preheat the oven, it is good to check the oven for the forgotten cookies you might have made last time and forgotten about.

Cheese Sauce

ok first melt about a fourth or a third of a stick of butter in a small pot. Then add a little bit of flour. I don't know how much, okay. Like about a fourth or a third of a scoop or so. Mix the flour with the butter until it is all smooth. Then add some milk. It's not really my business how much milk you add, okay. Maybe a half cup would be good but I feel that it is a decision that only you can make. Same with the grated cheese, which you will be adding next. Make sure the milk is heated pretty well before adding the cheese. Maybe about a cup would be good, but who is to say? Stir it until everything is smooth and melted. Now you have a cheese sauce that you can pour over some broccoli or maybe even some pasta. If you want to dip bread into it or eat it with a spoon, who am I to stop you.

Strawberry "Pie"

OK this is something yummy that tastes great with a little bit of ice cream. It is pretty easy to make but not that impressive or fancy. You're basically going to put a half or more stick of butter, a cup of sugar, and a couple of quarts of chopped up strawberries in a pot and heat it up and stir it until it is juicy and you taste it and it is yummy. Keep stirring it and heating it until there is a lot of strawberry juice mixture. Then you put it in a 2.5 quart casserole dish and then you put one of those Pillsbury pie crusts from the refrigerated section of the grocery store on top of it and heat it in the oven at 350 for 20 or 25 or 30 minutes. Those crusts are like those doughy crusts that you kind of want to eat plain. And you know what? You can eat some plain and no one will know. Because you are basically going to have to fold the crust a little to set it on top of the strawberry goop. I am telling you, this pie is so simple and so yummy, especially with some vanilla ice cream. It is kind of messy looking at first and people, when thy see it, might mock you or even slap you and they will try to say that you don't really know how to make a pie, and they will try to say that you don't even know what a pie is supposed to look like. But when they eat it, they will feel ashamed of themselves, which is the whole point of baking.

Easy Cheesecake

This cheesecake recipe probably isn't going to make you "famous for your cheesecake." But if you want to make a yummy little cheesecake that you can share with people who don't judge you, then buy yourself a shortbread or graham pie crust from the grocery store, mix up two packs of cream cheese, two eggs, 2/3 cup of sugar, and a teaspoon of vanilla, pour the mixture into the pie crust, and bake it at 350 for thirty minutes. I mean, that's all there is to it. Do you want to put some strawberries on it? Well then put some strawberries on it. Maybe mix the strawberries with some sugar first. or heat up the strawberries with sugar and maybe a little butter so there is kind of a strawberry sauce. When you serve it, it might be good to say something like, "I did the best I could, okay?"

Cherry Cheese Pie

Do you have an extra five minutes? Well maybe you could mix together one pack of cream cheese, a third of a cup of lemon juice, and a can of sweetened condensed milk and then put it in a shortbread pie crust and then top it with a can of cherry pie filling. Do you have a whole day? Well then maybe you could make 288 of these pies.

Grits Extravaganza

Have you ever heard southerners talk in such a southern accent that you don't know what they are saying? Well they are probably talking about grits. And basically what is so yummy is if you make some grits and divide the recipe in two and put cheese in some of the grits and then eat them and then put brown sugar in the other grits and then eat that for dessert. But the question is, how do you make the grits. Well I think it is yummy to use milk. Maybe skim milk, like 2 cups plus a cup of water, or maybe 3 cups of skim milk. It doesn't really matter because some people use only water! But milk is yummy so you can use milk. Bring the milk to a boil or just really hot. Then dump in about a cup of grits. Then keep stirring until it gets creamy. Then add a little bit of butter.

Easy Holiday Meal

Add some heavy cream to store bought gravy and mix it on the stovetop and it feels like you made it yourself. Serve with storebought rotisserie chicken and rice.

Today

I decided that the epilepsy treatment was just too expensive
and instead I bought some mystery fudge
from that guy in my neighborhood.

Sometimes poems are hard to understand

guys my seizure disorder
is the icing on the cake.
It really is.
All those cupcakes you see in New York
in all those little shops?
and the big cakes in the cases
and even the ice cream cakes at Dunkin Donuts-
all that icing on all those cakes is my seizure disorder.
And the punchline is dementia.

IQ poem

Yeah I did want to be the smartest person in my school
and I am not but some of the people smarter than me
eat their boogers.

poem from the walk home

I think it's cute when cartoon characters have stuffed animals.

I think the angels will write a history that people have to believe.

Funnel cake

Guys what if in heaven
there is a big funnel that blessings get poured into
before being distributed
and God and saints and angels
drop stuff like cakes and computers
and guinea pigs in for fun.

Or maybe

heaven might be so great that the sinkholes in landfills
are the funnels that blessings get poured into
before being distributed on earth.

Savings Plan

Maybe Judgment Day is when we find out
that we get to keep all the coins
from the curse jars in heaven.

A gift

Guys what if people in heaven are living in replicas of our apartments here possibly to pray for us or possibly to make fun of us. Today I am going to buy a new painting for my living room as a gift to them.

Poem

A fun game to play at the airport is guess what inappropriate thought I am thinking.

poem

I think when people turn 18
they should all check a box that says
they agree to terms and conditions
and then after that they should not have to sign anything else.

poem

guys there is no way to fully know
what happens
in the chemistry lab of Jesus Christ.
A little bit of this and a little bit of that
and before you know it
you have a job selling donuts to the PTA.

poem

I think the MSW licensing exam should be a one question test that says what is the 8th wonder of the world?
And then the answer is "the Diagnostic Statistical Manual of Mental Disorders"
and they have that answer written down on the back of the test.

poem

What if you were almost done with social work school and you realized you weren't very good at it and you decided to transfer and traded all your credits for one credit in a comedy certificate program?

poem

What if you were a therapist but anytime anyone tried to tell you anything you said
"That's none of my business."

poem

Jesus Christ never sinned
but if he had sinned
it would have been the perfect amount.

Toaster Strudel

life is hard guys
but maybe the person you marry will have a toaster.

Proposal proposal

sometimes people ask people to marry them in creative ways
but what is more creative than saying
will you be the one to always trim my pet guinea pigs toenails.

poem

it is not good
to say that flypaper
is the best thing
that ever happened to you
but wow.

Staying Alive

People in heaven will say
What is happening?
Maybe it is an earth prayer.

Ok I think I figured it out

The thought transcripts are on cells.
Entire brain records on cells that become dust
which stays in the atmosphere when the world explodes
and all the matter gets sucked into a vortex
and the people in space or in the future or heaven
collect all the dust in a giant container
and pour the dust into a funnel
connected to the movie machine
and then everyone watches everything on a screen
and all the thoughts are broadcast out loud.

The Last Judgment

In heaven maybe everyone will chuckle to themselves
and say I sure got them didn't I

Just a little joke guys

What if you always referred to everyone you know as rivals?

Trying to win

When we were playing Apples to Apples at the mental hospital
at Columbia Presbyterian
yeah I ended up saying that the Garden of Eden was expendable
a little joke about the fall of man I guess
gets em every time
saying everything's fine the way it is
and why be psychotic if you can't say stuff like that.

Posts from my Old Candy Reviews Blog:

Stork Chocolate Reisen: My Reisen For Living

Get it? Reisen? Reason? My reisen for living? Kind of like my reason for living? Yeah, it's pretty clever. And true, too. They haven't done studies yet, but when they do, studies will probably show that Storck Chocolate Riesen motivate people more than any other incentive in the world. I am actually thinking about making a hat that has a Storck Chocolate Riesen hanging just out of my reach. I think this will help me keep on going when I want to quit something. Really, there's not much I am willing to do without being promised a Storck Chocolate Riesen. In fact, this post is the way it is because no one has offered me a Storck Chocolate Riesen in exchange for improving it.

Lemon Jolly Ranchers: A Basic Human Right

Ok, everyone, it's time to organize. I don't know how you found out about us, but we need all the help we can get to bring lemon Jolly Ranchers back to the forefront of American culture. There is an evil and vast conspiracy that has tried to keep lemon Jolly Ranchers out of the main Jolly Rancher assortments, and we simply will not stand for it any longer. They can try to keep the lemon jolly ranchers confined to the rarely stocked passion fruit assortment, but they will not prevail. Our movement has been gaining strength. There are lemon jolly rancher loyalists everywhere, and we have been waiting for the right time to take action. This is it, people. If you are one of our enemies, a lemon Jolly Rancher prohibitionist, and you think that because you stumbled upon our secret communications that you can somehow put an end to our activism, think again, you blue raspberry traitor. Join us now while you still can. Also, if you have any good ideas for posters and chants and slogans, please let me know, because so far, all I can think of is "hey, whatever happened to lemon Jolly Ranchers? Those were my favorite kind."

Mike and Ikes: Probably The Cure For Cancer

I'm not just saying that because of their being kind of pill-shaped. Mike and Ikes are so delicious that they probably have healing powers. The yumminess alone will probably add ten years to your life. Factor that in with the modified corn starch, the carnuba wax, and the red #40, and you've pretty much discovered the remedy for most ailments. I'm actually surprised they're shelved in the candy section instead of the medicine section, and it's a wonder that they're sold over the counter at all. It seems like with all the debate about health care, someone would have realized the potential of what is clearly the solution to most of America's health woes. And yes, this post is indeed just an attempt to get my insurance company to pay for Mike and Ikes.

Ferrer Rocher Chocolates: I can quit anytime I want

Some people have crystal meth. I have Ferrer Rocher chocolates.

It is an expensive habit, but I justify it by remembering how much money I have saved by not being a collector of Rolls Royces. When Ferrer Rochers are not on sale, it's four dollars for a twelve pack. (You didn't think I would get the three pack, did you?) But they are worth every penny, and they are also worth all the weird looks you get when you're camping out in the Bilo parking lot for the after-Christmas 50% off sale. (It's best to get there on Christmas Eve so you can save your place through Christmas Day, too.) And yeah, I do miss spending Christmas with my family, but Ferrer Rocher chocolates are like family to me, too.

Reese's Pieces:
I put them in my backyard and E.T. never came

That movie, E.T., was just two big fat hours of false advertising. I don't know about you, but when I saw it, I perceived a very clear message: "If you put Reeses Pieces in your yard, a lovable alien will come be your friend." Well, I put Reeses Pieces in my backyard, and I am still waiting for E.T. to come make my toys fly around the room and drink my parents' beer and take me for a bike ride in front of the giant moon. E.T. has not sent me so much as a postcard, and I don't appreciate the false hope that people instilled in my heart. After years and years of waking up early to see if E.T. has gotten here yet, I have about given up and am trying to look at the bright side—more Reeses Pieces for me. I didn't really want to share any Reeses Pieces with that slimy, gray, geranium-obsessed extra terrestrial anyway. E.T. would probably just follow me around asking to use my phone and telling me to "Be good." That preachy little candy-moocher won't find any more Reeses Pieces in my yard. Next time, don't bother with the defibrillator, people.

P.S. E.T., if you are out there reading this, I'm just joking. Please come visit me.

Werther's Original: not just for old people

Many of you probably don't eat Werther's originals because you grew up watching Price is Right and Perry Mason and they would always play those Werther's Originals commercials and that kid would get a Werther's original from his grandma, and it seemed like only grandmas were allowed to buy them. It seemed like in the same way there's a drinking age, there was also a Werther's Original age, and it was somewhere up around 75 or so. I thought this for a long time, and I even had procedures done to help me age faster so I would be eligible to buy them. I also adopted children and then had them adopt some children so I could technically be a grandma. Then, I went to Hollywood and got a professional make-up artist to make me look 80. Then, I bought a walker. Finally, I went to the store to buy some Werther's originals. They were definitely worth all the trouble, but the people at the register didn't even card me. I later found out that you don't have to be old, or even a grandma. You don't have to be a member of AARP, you don't have to be getting social security, and you don't even have to watch Wheel of Fortune. They let anyone try Werther's originals. If you do self-checkout, no one even knows that you bought them.

The Road More Traveled

Two roads diverged in a yellow wood,
And totally content with not being able to travel both,
I chose the one more traveled,
The one that had a more beaten path,
Because come on, people,
If that many people traveled on it,
It must be going someplace good,
And sure enough,
It led to a fruit stand
And I bought some marmalade
And things turned out fine.

Definite Infinity

I walked through a department store yesterday and thought about another time that I had walked through a department store. Next time I walk through the store, I will make sure to think about last time. That way, I can some day walk through a department store thinking about the time I walked through the store thinking about the time I walked through the department store thinking about the other time I walked through a department store. I will touch infinity, like the time I stood in front of the three angled mirrors in a department store and saw my reflections reaching back for eternity. There were infinity selves staring back at me, copying every move I made, helping me understand things in the eternity department.

New Years poem

Guys it turns out a serving size of meringues is about 14
so I only ate about three servings and then the rest of them.

How about this?

How about your bad prayers get canceled out
and everyone gets a strawberry milkshake?

Definite Infinity

I walked through a department store yesterday and thought about another time that I had walked through a department store. Next time I walk through the store, I will make sure to think about last time. That way, I can some day walk through a department store thinking about the time I walked through the store thinking about the time I walked through the department store thinking about the other time I walked through a department store. I will touch infinity, like the time I stood in front of the three angled mirrors in a department store and saw my reflections reaching back for eternity. There were infinity selves staring back at me, copying every move I made, helping me understand things in the eternity department.

New Years poem

Guys it turns out a serving size of meringues is about 14
so I only ate about three servings and then the rest of them.

How about this?

How about your bad prayers get canceled out
and everyone gets a strawberry milkshake?

poem

It's called Christianity.
You might want to look up your face in the dictionary.

poem

What if every thousand years
the holy spirit moves across the earth
in a way that exactly matches the wind.

poem

something just about everyone can do
is stay alive until they die.

Blanks

300 questions on a neuropsych test is a lot
and all I really knew for sure
was that I believe in law enforcement,
I'm not scared of mice,
and I don't like being criticized.

This might be the best poem I have ever written.

What if you tried a chicken nugget sauce that was so good
you decided you wanted to eat some
to go with all the chicken you have ever eaten
so you drink three gallons of it.

chin scratch scratch

people think that a facial expression of wisdom is someone with their hand on their head looking intellectual but it is really the expression on your face when you make a ham sandwich for later.

Butter poem

What if at church when people share testimonies a lot of people talked about growing up in a house where they used margarine and not butter. I think that would really get me, everyone. Really though that little girl was me.

Poem

warm laundry

Poem

midnight at the laughing parlor

Frog Poem

If I learned one thing from the society
it's that a frog is a beating heart.

Poem

Now I know what schizophrenia feels like
because of the conspiracy simulating schizophrenia.

Poem

I showed up late with the donuts
as if to say "It's not that easy to bring donuts."
as if to say "I had to go back for more."
as if to say "I'm late with the donuts."

Maybe God is mad at me

Maybe God is mad at me
or maybe I am a little baby elephant named Peanut.

Poem

I have a lot of reasons to be happy right now
because today I am innocent
of all the sins I will commit
during the rest of my life.

Poem

when I beat Santa
and get called Santa saint.

Possible Titles

Diagnosed with normalism

The homecoming queen from Jesus Christ's high school

The only thing that's not a hoax

Why not give them a magic marble

I mean why not give them a magic marble. They will say that is weird and I will say what's weird is not wanting magical powers. Just joking I will say it costs four dollars now do you think its weird.

Admiral Action Figure

Guys what if you were so cool and you gave everyone you knew an Admiral Akbar action figure for Christmas. Well Jesus Christ really did try to give everyone an Admiral Akbar but people nailed him to a cross but then he gave everyone an Admiral Akbar anyway and I am going to tell everyone about it especially in space a long time from now when I meet the real Admiral Akbar.

Crutch

What if there was a Christmas Carol story
where instead of there being a greedy miser like Scrooge,
the Christmas ghosts visited someone
who was spending too much time with family and friends
and they told him to go get a job.

Cake break

Some friends are the kind of friends
where when you are with them
your guardian angel probably gets some time off.

Poem

What if you said thanks
every time the grocery store cashier
scanned a grocery.

Another idea for a game

It is a card game for 52 people
where each person gets a card
and the person who gets the five of clubs wins.

Yeah I feel bad

Guys you know you are jealous
if you go through the stages of grief
when something good happens to a friend.

poem

voila: imperfection.

poem

do animals vote in heaven

poem

what if there was a football draft for fans

new words

homefulness

soonicide

respectacle

Pollution

Brown air

Poem

I'm thinking of making a photo collection
of found meaningless juxtapositions
like when someone leaves some cookies in the produce section
or if there is some trash on the ground
and it is a piece of plastic and an aluminum can.

poem

Guys what if someone told you something bad that happened to them
and you say you know what, I did forget to pray for you

Coping Skills

Brave people sometimes use shields.

a prayer for the grocery store cashiers on snowy days

everyone hurries to get their snacks and drinks to settle down
but the cashiers feel the burden
and have to drive home later when it isn't safe.
But maybe some day when they aren't expecting it,
some special blessing will drift from heaven,
softly coating their life in a calming sparkle
as they sit quietly with a hot chocolate and some peace and promise
of milk and bread forever.

Three angel poems

What if some of the angels
have pet angel guinea pigs
and they sometimes let the guinea pigs
walk around in a room
and it gives people a peaceful feeling
without ever realizing why.

What if each prayer that people pray
makes there be one more bullet
for the angels' machine guns?

What if someone had a decorated war general guardian angel
and the other angels are like "Who is that person and why are they so important?"
and then one day that person does something really simple
and the important angel moves on and is replaced by a normal angel.

Stand-up comedy routine

Hi everyone I hope you're having a great day. If you're not, maybe you can watch some funny stand up comedy or something after listening to this.

I think joking about hopeless situations is sometimes a way to help people feel better so I thought we could talk about my job search. I thought one thing I might try to interview for is an activity therapist, where you can just play games at a hospital. So you basically get paid to play cards, plus whatever money you win from poker, which could be a lot because of insurance. I think that I could have a good resume for a job like that, and I could list all the games I have ever played, and maybe the names of the people I have beaten. They could be my references. I would need to tell the interviewer ahead of time that they will probably lie and say they beat me at scrabble and trivial pursuit but that is all part of the fun.

Probably one of the questions they will ask during the interview is do you ever let people win? I will say sure I let people win so they think they can beat me and then when there's money on it I go ahead and cash in I mean that could be a good for a hospital you know a lot of people don't pay their bills and I think having an activity therapist there who can help bring in some extra cash could really help out.

another question they'll probably ask is if I know how to lead bingo games.

and I'll say yeah if it is video poker machines.

They will say you're not talking about gambling are you

and I will say no I never table talk. that is how you get shot. I do not want to get shot in a hospital, you know. it's just too ironic. What I want is to challenge people to a hospital wide game of trivial pursuit, where the main question is what is your insurance number? If people get it right, I keep my job, you know?

And really in terms of gambling, what is more gambling than paying 500 dollars a month for insurance and then the hospital wins 55 thousand dollars when you have a seizure disorder.

That is really one of the main things that makes me worry about getting a job. Well that and the manic depression. I feel like it could help me do good work, though, like it could be very comforting to be in a hospital and someone says, Hi, I am your social worker. And your roommate. You know I mean that is 24 hour care in a certain way.

I feel like it's a service I cant ever provide, though, if I cant get through a job interview, which I really can't unless they let you wear what you want and bring a photo of what you know you should have worn, and maybe bring someone else's resume so they know you know what a good employee would be like.

Missing

Poppy the Chihuahua went missing in my neighborhood
and when I see all the other dogs
I know one of them could be Poppy in disguise.

poem

Dreams do come true
and in some ways
it does rain coca cola
because of the way
you can buy a lot of it
at the store.

poem

I think a great pen name would be Victor Hugo.

Poem

It is very rare for guinea pigs to lick people's faces

But Roger does that

And why shouldn't he

And why shouldn't everyone

Please stop hurting me

poem

What if they do a scan of my brain
And they find a whole pack of M and Ms in there?

Echo

i had a terrible dream
but my dog from childhood
showed up at the end
and comforted me.

And I started wondering if in heaven or space somewhere
everyone's dreams are all lined up with actual physical settings
and if Echo my dog walked thousands of miles to be in that
dream for me.

And I wondered if earth was already like that
and that is why Echo was in my memory
right at the right time
wanting to be petted
maybe for my comfort
and maybe for Echos.

Pretty funny for a country to call themselves great in their own name

My last poem will be about
what happens
when the reputation of the British Empire crumbles
and the glistening shards melt into each other
and create googly eyed prism blobs singing
Glory, glory to the lamb
and join in the chorus
with all the other colorful shards
from all the other marytered names
shattered by dull and blunt rumor hammers.
I am not writing that poem yet,
because what if I am wrong
and should wait until I also escape time.

World Map

I was just looking at the world map
and started thinking that
for most people to pretty much agree
that all those countries are in fact
the countries as they are labeled
with the boundaries they have in the continents they are in
is really a huge agreement among a lot of people
and quite a treaty.

Crusade

I don't know why I got marked down on ethics
in my teaching program
but I think it might have been because of the presentation I gave
when I was asked what was the difference
between Islam and Christianity
and all I could think of was that Muslims don't eat bacon.
I mean maybe that came across wrong
but Christianity really is about eating bacon sometimes
and getting marked down on ethics for saying so.

Announcement

The cubes have been replaced.

The lost stone of prosperity has been recovered.

The antidote has been delivered.

The evil forest has burned down.

The bullet has been removed.

The ancient city has been discovered.

The midnight flight has succeeded.

Mission 4859 has been accomplished.

The new product line has been rolled out.

Fifi has been fired.

The mystical ice lake has thawed.

The torch of doom has been snuffed out.

Someone brought donuts.

The fifteenth lock has been unlocked.

The code has been cracked.

The case of the missing coordinate link has been solved.

The fleet has made it to the isle of the hidden silver moon treasure.

The passage to the magic harvest field has been found.

We have the day off next Monday.

The sword of crystal tides has sliced through the destructive mist.

The haze is gone.

The bad people have left.

The stairwell on mystery mountain is complete.

The dollar mart is having a grand opening.

The key to the hallway of doors is back in the secret bookshelf place.

The darkness blocking the fountain has been destroyed.

The waters of restoration have filled the pools.

The light has triumphed.

Free hamsters for everyone.

poem

What if you wrote one good research paper that was very general and you turned it in for all your classes you ever took for a whole degree.

poem

What if you had a friend who was always there for you and listened to everything you had to say and helped you with all your problems and then one day you needed some cash so you sued them for practicing therapy without a license.

poem

you cant just decide to believe
that you got a hundred on your spelling test
graded by the Lord Jesus Christ.
Either you did or you didn't
and you're probably lying and
there were probably some very complicated words on there
and you robbed a bakery anyway
so why do you think
being good at spelling
is going to solve all your problems
especially if they're math problems.

poem

if I am out of bounds maybe I got pushed out of bounds.

A Cloud of Glory

A cloud of privilege to hide the suffering

A cloud of suffering to hide the gift

A cloud of gift to hide the work

A cloud of work to show the love.

poem

Guys, dirty people might be dirty
because they are eating a piece of cake
that God gave them.

Refried Bean is from Greenville, SC.
Refried worked in a bookstore for twelve years
and has an M.F.A. in Writing
from Vermont College of Fine Arts.
Refried has three pet guinea pigs named
Fred, Roger, and Dave.